ORIGINS AND SOLUTIONS TO AFRICA'S

REBEL CONFLICTS

(The Sierra Leone Chapter)

Politicians Centred Approach

MOHAMED SANNOH

Methodist Boys' High School, Kissy Mess Mess, Freetown, Sierra Leone

Order this book online at www.trafford.com
or email orders@trafford.com

Most Trafford titles are also available at major online book retailers.

Printed in the United States of America.

ISBN: 978-1-4907-0981-9 (sc)
ISBN: 978-1-4907-0983-3 (hc)
ISBN: 978-1-4907-0982-6 (e)

Library of Congress Control Number: 2013913716

Trafford rev. 07/27/2013

 www.trafford.com

North America & international
toll-free: 1 888 232 4444 (USA & Canada)
fax: 812 355 4082

Contents

Introduction

"Africa is a great and the richest continent on the planet earth". This is the actual fact, even Britain and America cannot deny. Africa also suffers more than any other continent on this planet earth; but why is that and why are there more beggars on this same continent than any other continent on the planet earth? Despite the uncountable wealth in Africa, why are their governments always busy with looking for sustainable aids to support life sustenance in their countries? What are the causes and solutions to Africa's sufferings? Are we able to solve these problems? Do we always expect other people from different parts of the earth to solve our problems for us? The major and extreme form of Africa's problems now-a-days is the Civil War as a result of rebel conflicts emerging from countries to countries on the African planet.

This book is about explaining to readers, some major causes and solutions to Africa's problems, especially those relating to rebel conflicts. I will also attempt to research major origins and solutions to the causes of Africa's suffering, artificial poverty and many other causes that have pushed educated Africans in general, far away from the continent into refugee status in other continents of the planet earth.

Some countries, such as Sierra Leone, Liberia, Ivory Coast, Angola, Sudan-South Sudan, Uganda and Libya are mentioned in this context as case studies to justify my claims and also to authenticate the readers understanding of what I talk about. Other international organisations such as the United Nations Organisation (UNO), Economic Community of West African States (ECOWAS) etc. are mentioned but only to justify their roles in solving arm conflicts in some countries that are mentioned. I am a native of the West African state of Sierra Leone where one of the worst human catastrophes in the name of civil war in

Africa's history occurred from 1991 to 2002, under the rebel conflict leadership of my brother, Foday Sankoh. This human calamity on my country was strongly supported by Charles Taylor, the then President of Liberia as the Hague proved him guilty. As I write this book in my student flat at University of Abertay Dundee in Scotland, I am still finding difficult to stop my tears because I will ever remain to miss my school mates and large number of my extended families whom I will never meet alive on my arrival in my Eastern Province village of Bongor Koya as a result of being killed in the Sierra Leone civil war. If there are questions to ask, I will be tempted to ask my brother Foday Sankoh the following:

Why did my brother start the rebel war? How long did he plan to do this? Did he gain any benefit for Sierra Leone? Did he gain personal benefits for doing this? Did the people of Sierra Leone learn any sense from this? Will another civil war occur again in Sierra Leone?

I am trying to find answers to these questions in this book.

Mohamed Sannoh, University of Abertay Dundee, Scotland

CHAPTER ONE

Causes of civil conflicts in Africa— Politicians Corruption

Many people have their own definitions of civil war but what I personally refer to as civil war is basically fighting of armed conflicts to a high level that causes citizens of the same county to fight with each other; either basing from differences of political party, tribal, religious, sexual or land ownership.

The major causes of civil war resulting into brothers fighting brothers, especially in Africa is due to greed. What is greed? This is situation of the mind that causes an individual to be in control of all and to claim all for him or herself even when they do not need all to survive. The basic need of human nature to survive is the ability to have food, shelter and clothing.

As long as these basic wants are satisfied, one must give chance to others to have their own basic needs. But most people, especially in Africa, like to have more than what they need to survive and they even enjoy other people suffering in their neighbourhoods while they have many to lavish to the admiration of those without. It is common for rich men to drive very expensive cars living in very expensive houses up the street in a less privileged environment with haggard streets but those without see them passing by with envy and to their satisfaction because they can afford more than anyone in the area. They can afford to have generators in their compounds to supply electricity wile their neighbourhoods in darkness.

They take it as privilege for their neighbours who cannot afford televisions to come to their homes to watch their TV programmes. They prefer their children to attend expensive private schools and driven to schools in expensive cars on a daily basis while other children from less privilege parenthoods walk to high populated schools in single uniforms on a daily basis and even without shoes, but on bare feet. Never the less, children of these less parenthoods are even just privileged to find themselves in schools at all. What happens more in such cases is that the so called privilege people are politicians living in the neighbourhoods. Sometimes it sounds as a natural punishment for a poor man to live in a neighbourhood with a politician such as a member of parliament or a cabinet minister of an African government.

They behave as if the country in which they live belong to them alone and their voting into government is license for them to loot and squander the nation's wealth and lavish on womanising, drunkenness and show-offs that are very unnecessary but just to get poor people angry and to the extent of getting them to the understanding that something is not right and it is about time to correct these wrongs. The powers of politics is so high in Africa that even when journalists attempt to call attention of politicians to the sensitivities of their behaviours of injustice, they either do not care or they exercise their political powers to arrest those journalists and send them to jail for a period of time. It is also very uncommon to hear of African governments auditing their government ministers to account for specific spending of amount of government money that belongs to tax payers. As far as Africa is concerned, a government minister that supports a ruling party in government does no wrong. All amount of money that comes to their possessions meant for covering expenditure in their ministries for the purpose of developments and for the benefits of tax payers in the country remains on calculator to divide how much goes to their ministry's projects and how much goes into their overseas bank account. If for example, the amount of £10million is given to the Minister of Health for the development of hospital equipments in two hospitals, the very first they do is to divide that amount into equal halves of £5million straight.

They then puts £2million in a suitcase and walk with it to the president; give him thanks and pledge their continuous supports for the party and sends the other £3million into their overseas bank account. This means that the £10million approved for the ministry's expenditure remains £5million only to cater for the two hospitals which will not be enough and they are not asked to produce receipts of expenditure in authentic audits for their spending. If the government audits forces any other auditing moves, they will receive a phone call from the president that ministry expenditure is ok and approved.

When information of such conversation from the president is revealed by any news paper, the publisher gets arrested and put in jail because that is where he belongs for publishing the presidential communication without his permission. In a civilised world like Britain, that is referred to as corruption and no elements of it, is tolerated in their politics. We have seen government ministers and party politicians sacked from their positions in British politics for claiming small amounts of money as low as £50 more that what they are expected. Within the frameworks of African politics, the major calamity is tribalism. What is tribalism? Tribalism is when two people belong to two different tribes, speaking two different languages of two different regions in the same country.

In an imaginary African state like Bulayngay there are fifteen different tribes including the Zumarkis and five others in the North and the Balajos and seven others in the South. The present head of state is a Zumarkis man, which makes power to be in the North because the tribal division is that the country has the Zumarkis in the North and the Balajors in the South. Where the Minister of Education is a Zumarkis by tribe, the offer university places and offer of scholarships to study at the university will heavily be channelled towards the Zumakis and the northerner tribal applicants even when the Balajos and other southerner tribal applicants are more qualified. This explains that the politics of the day favours to develop the Zumarkis tribe.

This is also another form of corruption in African politics and these kinds of corruptions are very highly institutionalised to the point that those who don non come from areas of the country where the political powers are not balanced are left to accept that it is not yet their time to benefit from the politics of their countries.

Therefore, if you ask me in a nutshell to tell you the causes of rebel conflicts in Africa, **the answers I will give to your question are "CORRUPTION! CORRUPTION and CORRUPTION!"** especially those instituted by our politicians and expect us to accept as way of life and the origin of this corruption is greed. Politicians want to have everything, eat everything including foods, money and beautiful women. Those who are greedy always expect everything for themselves and show white teeth and very niece affectionate appearance to cheer up the needy.

They pretend to us to be caring but they keep themselves busy with squandering the nation's wealth for their own personal pockets. They use our monies to top up their overseas bank accounts and these bank accounts are so secured that no one has access to it, even when they die.

Such amount of money therefore stays with the foreign banks to benefit the countries in which they are. Our government ministers buy houses in developed overseas countries and send their children there to study in advanced universities while their nations educational institutions are left impoverished but the question again here is, what do they actually benefit from this? "What good is it for a man to gain the whole world, yet forfeit his soul?" This is a very old biblical question that Disciple Mark of Our Lord Jesus Christ asked in verse 36 of Chapter 8 of his gospel. What excuse do they have on the day of judgement?

Is rebel conflict the way out?

I don't think any decent civilised person prefers civil conflict as solution to problems they are not able to solve. However, when human sufferings continues to the level so long, it reaches to a point where all conditions become unbearable, especially where these conditions become daily occurrence to the permanent and especially where the leaders do not recognised the signs and warnings of the suffering public. As a result of being fed up, they are left with no alternative but to strike into civil conflict, as they already have nothing to loose. "He that is down fears no fall" is a common saying of the suffered.

Examples of civil conflicts we can learn from

Africa has suffered from chains of civil conflicts which are discussed to educate our current and future politicians with the expectation of behaving properly to protect their countries.

i.   *The Sierra Leone civil war*
ii. *The Liberia civil war*
iii. *The Uganda civil war*
iv. *The Somali civil war*
v.   *The Democratic Republic of Congo civil war*
vi. *The Angola civil war*

CHAPTER TWO

Origin of the Sierra Leone civil war

The West African state of Sierra Leone is one of the African countries that have recently experienced human catastrophe on the surface of the planet earth. Why and how did this war happen in such a very rich, prosperous and peaceful country?

It has taken me a decade to discover the cause of the Sierra Leone civil war. In other words, to find out why did my brother Foday Sankoh start the civil war? I recalled a TV interview of Foday Sankoh by a Gambian BBC journalist Ebrima Sillah in the year 2001.

I can still recall from this interview that my brother, Foday Sankoh's idea for civil war in Sierra Leone did not come up within a day and start immediately. It was a fermented seed that was sewn in 1967 by the then President Siaka Stevens of Sierra Leone when he planned the abuse power to the point of forcing one party rule on the country in 1978, abusing the nation's wealth through stealing and saving in foreign bank accounts, leaving Sierra Leoneans to suffer for basic necessities, including the staple food of rice. At the time things were getting more difficult for Sierra Leoneans in their own country, Siaka Steven was boasting of having hotels he bought in places like Las Palmas which created employments for other people in different country.

To worsen the situation, Siaka Stevens left Joseph Siadu Momoh in charge that he transferred power to as President of Sierra Leone in 1985 and we all went into singing for him in the streets of Freetown saying:

"Who da gie Momoh power? Na God!

Who da gie Momoh power? Na God!

Momoh nor worry na God don put you there,

Water way na for you-o, e-nor go run pass you.

Water way na for you-o, e-nor go run pass you".

Remember, Momoh was never voted for by the voters but transferred power to who immediately became power chief in the country under the one party banner of All Peoples Congress (APC). Why did Siaka Stevens transferred power to Momoh and not to his Vice President, Sorie Ibrahim Koroma?

What did S.I.Koroma do that forfeited him the presidency at State House in Sierra Leone after all the evils he introduced in Sierra Leone politics in total supports of Siaka Stevens individually and the APC as a political party in general? S.I. left no evil unturned as he went to the extend of labelling himself "Agba Satan" the agent of Satan the devil, and no one can mess with him and get away.

Why did he allow himself to be used by Siaka Stevens and APC to that level? Was it due to ill health at that time from car accident he encountered at that time that he was not appointed president?

The whole country went into pocket debates in corners that Siaka Stevens was protecting his life by making sure that the army chief will not prosecute him by bringing him to justice to account for all he did during his misrule of power and human right abuse.

My brother Foday Sankoh also revealed in that same interview that Sierra Leoneans were for a long time braising themselves for the civil war by saying openly in the street that unless war happens in this country, we cannot learn our lesson and the politicians will not stop sizing advantage on us.

When J.S. Momoh became president of Sierra Leone under the one party "democracy", his popularity was very high as he started with the introduction of price control especially on basic commodities including staple foods. The problem that emerged immediately with this popularity was the implementation; as there was no backup strategy in place to support the price control system and immediately, his total image of himself started coming out as he was proved to be a total disgrace to himself, to the political party he represented (All Peoples Congress-APC) and Sierra Leone in particular.

He proved to be a drunkard and a womaniser to the point of not picking, even under aged girls for his sexual urge at Lagoonda night club near Cape Sierra Hotel at Lumbley beach in the West end of Freetown. In most occasions, he enjoyed himself there to the point of falling on the floor helplessly. Momoh was so useless to the extend that the tribal people among the Fulani's who wanted to break through into Sierra Leone and get away with corruption bribed him with virgins to have sex with which he accepted with pleasure. Is this the kind of leader my country should have at any time? My brother, Foday Sankoh did not think so.

CHAPTER THREE

Taste of the Mende culture

Originated from the Northern Province among the Limba people who was recruited in the Sierra Leone Military Forces (SLMF) by Siaka Stevens and eventually moved to settle down in Freetown during his military service, my brother Foday Sankoh narrowly escaped execution for the failed coup d'état for which Sieka Stevens killed Mohamed Sorrie Forna and fourteen others; he could have been included, which he knew about well in advanced but escaped. He could have been charged with "misprision of treason" which is also severally punishable with life imprisonment according to the constitution of Sierra Leone. He felt that his life was very risky. he no longer felt safe in Freetown and he changed address but did not go to his Limba line in the North. He moved to the far Eastern Province and settled in one of the boarder villages near the Segbwema Township where he established himself as photographer among the Mende/Kissy tribal people and closer to Liberia. My brother Foday Sankoh found his new village settlement address very strategic for his rebel war planning.

As a photographer, he embarked on moving from village to village and the border townships in both Sierra Leone and Liberia in search of photographing business, taking pictures of people and washing them in Segbwema and taking them back to their owners at affordable prices. Names of those who could not afford to pay at his arrival were taken and negotiated with them to have their pictures and pay him back upon his next arrival, say in two weeks time. He became very popular among these tribes and regarded him as a businessman that can understand his customers.

This movement was also a spying plot which gave him the opportunity to understand the areas properly including all the bye-ways and the bye-passes in the Eastern Province and the Western Liberia counties of Lofa, Gbarpolu and Grand Cape Mount. He was also smart enough to learn and pick up quickly the Mende/Kissy tribal languages and the major part of their cultures.

Mende people are the largest of the tribes of the thirteen tribal groups in Sierra Leone although the current APC government has politically falsified the tribal statistics to create more political constituencies in the Northern Province for political gains and vote riggings. My brother Foday Sankoh clearly understood that the Mende people in general are very open minded especially to strangers as long as their wives are not tampered with for personal love making pleasure purposes. That is the worst crime any stranger can commit to a Mende man and especially in his own locality that he cannot accept. No man can come from outside for sex tourism holidays in the Mende settlements of Sierra Leone. Although friendly and kind in nature, strangers in Mende land are always accepted with caution until they proved their decency to satisfaction.

If they are not satisfied beyond reasonable doubts, they will ask you to leave their village immediately because they don't want to be held responsible for anything that may happen to you.

When strangers move into their settlements, they are not allowed to stay there immediately all by themselves. They have to establish a host to stay with who could be a well known citizen of the area and he will be the one that can introduce the stranger to the village chief as his guest. He will further be responsible for any form of mischievousness that the stranger may get involved in and if he runs away, his guest will be held responsible to pay all the fines. When it is time to banish the stranger out, the host is contacted immediately. Women are not allowed to serve as stranger's host, because they may not unknowingly handle their behaviours that may come up in future and secondly the seriousness of the severe punishment may not be extended to women.

If you want to be genuinely generous to a Mende-man's wife, you have to go through the husband for the presentation of your generosity to his wife; otherwise you will be in trouble if the wife tells her husband that you (a stranger) have extended some kind of generosity to her without knowledge of her husband first. The husband will sue you immediately to the village chief and request that you go away from there immediately, without sleeping there for another night. When a Mende-man notices that you fancy his wife, you are classed as a time bomb in the waiting, to cause danger to mankind.

No woman is allowed to live in a Mende village without a husband for fear that men sexual desires may cause fighting over her; but sometimes, there are single women who might have lost their husbands as a result of natural deaths. *Although divorce happens among the Mendes, it is not very common among them. Mende women fear divorce very highly, especially when they have children in their marriages. The reason for this is that they protect their children with blessings they get from their husbands in the marriage. Mende husbands are considered as parents to their wives whom they live to protect and care for throughout their lives. Mende women are also fear of not creating stumbling blocks on their children's own marriages in future. That makes their community very unique*

If a stranger falls in love with a woman, especially if she is a matured single woman in the village, he will genuinely asked his host to approach her parents or relatives on his behalf and ask for her hands in marriage, but the woman will only agree to such marriage proposal provided that stranger decides to settle down permanently in her Mende village.

The dowry is paid and she becomes legally his wife before sexual intercourse takes place between the two. The dowry costs only three pennies (tro-pence), although you are also free to extend other generosities to the extended members of the wife's family to any large amount you can afford.

Once a Mende woman is married to her man, he will not get into sexual relationship with any of her wife's extended family members again, although the rest of her relatives will continue referring to him as their husband jokingly.

The Mende people are very concern about keeping their community clean and they always take due regard of their community laws seriously. It is always very common to get a sermon in the village court for stealing when you root out a cassava from a roadside to quench temporary hunger relief. The only solution is to ask for it from the owner who will be kind enough to give to a hungry man and get blessings from the Almighty God in Heaven. Men who beat up their wives always find themselves in big trouble of heavy fines from the village chief as a point of teaching him a lesson to always control his temperament especially when dealing with his wife or any other female.

Mende people are referred to as "Natural Born Lawyers" because they always immediately get their witnesses first and thereafter sue in courts. Their legal minded awareness in anything they do always make it difficult to socialise with other tribes, especially the Temnes, who are known to believe in fighting to settle down misunderstanding, but the Mende people believe in court settlements and heavy fines of their offenders. Most strangers who do business in the Mende settlements end up spending all their savings in court fines and leave empty handed because the Mende people know how to collect evidence and get ready for court summons.

One has to be careful with gesturing with a Mende-man's wife. He will not appreciate very much when his wife is hugged and kissed on her cheek, especially by someone he does not know personally. He will take up the matter with his wife and accuse her of having affair with that man and then forces her to call her name on love affairs which should be taken to court to pay fine. Never, ever touch a Mende woman's breast even when both of you are joking together; otherwise, she will call your name to her husband as touching her feelings and that is punishable in court with heavy fines.

CHAPTER FOUR

The Mende weddings

Now, let me touch a bit on how a young Mende lady and a young man get wed in the Mende settlement for the first time. The parents are always careful and sceptical with confirming allowance to their children in entering into first marriages.

For a Mende young man, for example, to get married for the first time to a young lady with no marriage experience, the young lady at first takes to introduce him to her parents (mum and dad) for handshakes. The young man, by nature is always very nervous at this first meeting but the young lady's dad will reassure him with a welcome smiles and ask, how are your parents doing? That question is very important as it always try to find out whether they are living together as married couples (husband and wife) at the time he has developed interests in their daughter. The dad will again send regards to his parents when he is leaving and with assurance that he will be pleased to meeting them in the not too distance future.

Thereafter, the young man will then introduce the girl to his parents where it is assumed that the young lady is not known to them. The young-man's dad will immediately ask for her parents (mum and dad) for the same reason. Thereafter the young-lady will spend some times with the young-man's mother. This time is focused on interviewing the young-lady to find out whether her parents (mum and dad) are still together as husband and wife at the time their son has developed interest in their daughter. After this interview meeting the mum, she will report to the young-man's father what she finds out. The dad will also be interested to know that their daughter is still a virgin and has not given herself up sexually to her new found love before their proposed wedding.

They will then call their daughter and give her a feedback of their opinions about the young-man she introduced to them. If they discover that the young-man's parents (mum and dad) are divorced and are no longer together as husband and wife at the time, they will not be happy and pleased to give a total approval of her interest in getting married to such a young-man; for the reason that divorce already exist in his family and if he is to inherit that, the possibility for him of kicking her out for another woman in future already exist and this will not be in the interest of their daughter. That shows that he comes from a family that do not have serious regard for marriages and divorce does not mean anything to him. The mum will then have a personal discussion with her daughter such as these:

"we really want you to be very happy but we are also concerned about your future, especially when we are not alive and be around to continue loving you. Remember my daughter, no one loves you more than the way we love you, but nature dictates that you should get married and start a family of your own you are to live with for the rest of your life. We as your parents have the responsibility to guide you well in making your choice of husband; even though we do not force a choice on you. When the right person comes for you, all signs will be cleared and therefore, please my daughter, wait for Mr. Right and don't rush into marriage".

However, if they still love each other and wants to get married, they can go ahead to take the risk but they (her parents) will not be present and will not take part in the wedding ceremonies, because it is not considered as being cleaned in sight of the Almighty God who blesses all weddings. The only way out is for the young man to meet his parents and ask them to reconcile together as married couples at that time, so that he cannot miss his love. If they really love their child, they will take this request seriously to make him happy as he was not responsible for their divorce.

It is always very difficult for a Mende young man to marry a woman who has already divorced-out of her first marriage, even if she is very beautiful and sexy. Mende people see the beauty of a woman from inside and not from outside even if she has a body shape like a mermaid with her lips like Whitney Houston and a remarkable shaky bottom. How could this tradition be managed especially dealing with Mende children born and brought-up in UK now-a-days, is the nightmare of all Mende parents that have migrated here.

Another very interesting fact about the Mende-man is that he has the right to sue his wife to the town chief if she refuses to have sex with him at a time she is not on her menstruation or sick otherwise. Failing to have sex with her husband means that she is seeing another man in secret and he will demand that she calls his name and when she finally does, the wife's boyfriend named will be heavily fined and for bidden from seeing her again, otherwise he will be exiled from the village indefinitely.

Having a Mende-woman girl friend

The Mende woman values herself so much that it is very difficult or almost impossible for her to propose love to a man even if she is madly in love with him. She will demonstrate with gestures for the man to understand that she has fallen in love and if he makes his move, he has a better chance to score. The Mende women believe that it is only prostitutes that rush on men because they are only after sex and if they rush, they are never taken seriously by the man as being reliable. It is also difficult for Mende women to engage into sexual fling especially with a man they do not know and have not met before, regardless of how hot and honey they might be at the time.

They prefer men that are introduced first by someone they know well. When a man proposes to a Mende woman, she will never say yes on the sport but **"if she smiles and say leave me alone because you are not serious"**, the man stands a better chance but will not push hard at this time. If the man pushes too hard at that time, she will conclude that he is only after her knickers.

She will tell you **"give me chance to think over"**. What you can then do is to get her a gift of niece perfume wrapped in a white handkerchief. That is what they all value most in establishing love making (not very serious one) relationship. *"Make sure you don't break my heart"* is the final warning for you to know that she has agreed and accept you as alright.

Once a Mende woman says ok to a man she means it for life and her commitment is always 100% in every thing she does to her man. She therefore expects total satisfaction from her boyfriend in everything. So when you are meeting her for the first time, she will make sure to cook very well so that you eat properly and become very strong. The best thing to do as a man is to chew kola nut with ginger root, two hours before your meeting, to give you the Viagra spell that activate your manhood into a "two in one horse-power-mood" to make sure that she does not take control over you.

That is why other tribesmen in Sierra Leone fight hard to get a Mende woman girlfriend. They are expert in love making. A Mende woman is naturally proud and does not like making frequent requests on her boyfriend in the act of avoiding disrespect.

Instead, she takes prides in feeding the boyfriend well at all times because she has the belief that all men are like children and they will grow to love women more when they are well fed at all times. However, what they appreciate more is gifts, even when not expensive ones.

Polygamy in the Mende culture

Polygamy is practiced in almost every African culture including that of the Mendes in Sierra Leone. By definition, polygamy is the practice of a man having more than one wife in his household. Why is this culture practice in Sierra Leone, especially by the Mende people? They do this for reasons that they are farmers and a man having many wives will have large number of labourers to work in the farm. Secondly, they will be able to have many children to contribute to the farm work and continuously contribute to the human population. As greater part of Mende settlements are Muslims, polygamy is also practiced for religious rights. What ever the reason might be, I think it is due to individual likeness for pleasure with different women.

My late father Karmoh Keifala Sannoh had only one wife, Yea Massah Komeh Sannoh and he was the Chief Imam in charge of twenty mosques in twenty villages in the Koya chiefdom where I was born. He had all excuses to have different wives but he only loved and preferred to have my mother alone. God bless them!

Polygamy is common among chiefs in villages of Mende settlements to have many children and it is also very common for an elderly chief of sixty years old to accept a twenty years old young-lady in marriage when he already has children around the ages of thirty. One may usually be tempted to ask, *"is he strong enough to serve his new wife in bed properly?"* especially when he has a couple of about three of such young ladies, with age similarities as wives. What is more interesting is when such young ladies continuously become pregnant and having children.

My own marriage to my lovely wife, Sao Sannoh has lasted for 26 years at the time of writing this book and we have four children. I am not ready or planning on having another wife anyway. I am only disappointed when she has told me that she has got tired of having children when we initially agreed on ten children during our romance days in 1986. However, it is still not too late to adopt six\more children from the Mende land because I just feel good with children around me.

Through careful studies, it has been proved that most of those children of the chiefs are not biologically his, although they all carry the surname of the chiefs whose wives give birth to these children.

The hidden facts about such children are that when older men have young wives, they attract young men who will be meeting with the young ladies in exchange for free labour in the farms of their husbands.

This arrangement will also be well known to their husbands who say nothing but give blind eyes as if nothing is happening, as long as they are getting free labour in their farms.

This secret remains in the family until when the chief dies and the search for successor comes up when his children comes up to defend their legitimacy. That will be the time when their true father is revealed publicly to even the very children and also to the general public.

CHAPTER FIVE

Civil war starts in Sierra Leone

In March 1991, my brother, Foday Sankoh started the civil war in Sierra Leone under the umbrella of his movement he called "Revolutionary United Front (RUF)" which commenced with a campaign against President Momoh's A.P.C government, capturing towns on border with Liberia. One may not be surprised because he had already been living there and planning his war strategies.

The war became so brutal that many townships and villages fell into rebel hands and families displaced to the level of not knowing where about family members including children, parents, brothers and sisters. I was in Sunderland University by then and an African friend of mine on the same course in the same class, Henry Mutumba from Uganda whose country has experienced civil war before and under Idi Amin Dada told me that the rebel war that has started in your country is not very good news because it cannot end up in a hurry. It will also affect so many things you have worked for all these years and many innocent people will die as a result.

The Formation of United Nations Mission in Sierra Leone (UNAMSIL)

On 22 October 1999, the Security Council established United Nations Mission in Sierra Leone [UNAMSIL] to cooperate with the Government and the other parties in implementing the Lome Peace Agreement and to assist in the implementation of the disarmament, demobilization and reintegration plan. On 7 February 2000, the

Council revised UNAMSIL's mandate. It also expanded its size, as it did once again on 19 May 2000 and on 30 March 2001.

According to the global security report (www.globalsecurity.org) the internal conflict involved multiple ethnic groups and resulted in an estimated 15,000 deaths from 1991 through 1996. By early 1999 estimates of the number of dead in the rebel war ranged upward from 50,000. At different times estimates of the number of displaced people were as high as 2.5 million—more than half of the entire population.

As many as half a million persons fled to neighbouring countries to escape the civil conflict, and remain outside the country on their own or in refugee camps, primarily in Guinea and Liberia. Many Sierra Leoneans went to seek refuge as far as to other African states of The Gambia, Guinea Bissau, Senegal and Ghana. The Sierra Leonean refugee stories from those who camped in neighbouring Guinea Conakry wasn't pleasant as they were opened to a high level of abuse and a series of harassments from the Guinean police forces.

Of all the West African states, the Republic of The Gambia proved to be more welcoming and homely because Sierra Leonean refuges experienced some freedoms they never experienced in their own country. They had opportunity to even establish their own businesses that competed freely with the local ones. President Yahya Jammeh was also very accommodating and extended high level of humanitarian supports to the Sierra Leonean refugees as they contributed very highly on the development of education in all sectors.

Over 250,000 citizens crossed the borders of Guinea and Liberia to escape the conflict; many thousands of others were displaced internally, and fled their homes to hide in wooded areas, or to towns where there are security forces and some degree of protection from rebel forces.

The conditions that existed in Sierra Leone made it vulnerable to a person like my brother, Foday Sankoh, leader of the Revolutionary United Front, to gather up disenfranchised young people who had not been paid for a long time. Over a period of twenty years, the central government gradually disintegrated as a result primarily of the political class, as they would say in Sierra Leone, eating everything in the government. Over a period of time, they destroyed the ability of the government to rule, to govern, and to do anything on behalf of the people. They stopped years ago paying civil servants or teachers. And when the centre disintegrated the entire periphery went its own way.

And people felt that they could not change this society through the political process because it had been compromised through the one-party state and through corruption which Joseph Saidu Momoh encouraged very highly through womanising and drunkenness. So you see, Siaka Stevens seed of corruption which did not take accountability as government policy by saying *"wu sie den tie cow na dae e for eat."* (Where they tie cow is where it must graze) became more aggravated and went out of control. Corruption and vote rigging are the major parts of legacies Sieaka Stevens left with the APC in Sierra Leone.

Foreign involvement in the Sierra Leone conflict is a serious problem, and there is clear evidence that Liberia and Burkina Faso are supporting the rebel efforts. Sierra Leone's participation in the West African peace-keeping force, ECOMOG, that went into Liberia that provoked Charles Taylor's retaliation against Sierra Leone. Charles Taylor, now the president of Liberia, saw that intervention as hostile to him when he was fighting for power there. They also had the support of Libya, which sent weapons to them through Burkina Faso which were then transshipped overland through the Ivory coast, through Liberia, into Sierra Leone.

The diamond mining industry provides the rebels with potential revenue of approximately $300 million per year. Precisely how much is spent on small arms and ammunition is unknown. What is known is that arms are apparently procured in Eastern Europe and staged through Burkina Faso and then continue on to Liberia for eventual delivery to rebel forces in Sierra Leone.

Sierra Leone is an extremely poor country. Before the civil war began in 1992, more than 70 percent of the 4.5 million citizens were involved in some aspect of agriculture, mainly subsistence farming. Although the country has substantial mineral resources, including diamonds, gold, rutile, and bauxite, official receipts from legal exports have been small in recent years. For decades the majority of diamond and gold production has been smuggled abroad. The economic infrastructure has nearly collapsed due to corruption, neglect, and war-related disruptions. The 6-year RUF insurgency dislocated more than 40 percent of the country's population, placing additional burdens on Sierra Leone's fragile economy.

Eighteen ethnic groups make up the indigenous population of Sierra Leone. The Temne in the north and the Mende in the South are the largest. About 60,000 are Creoles, descendants of freed slaves who returned to Sierra Leone from Great Britain and North America. Sierra Leoneans were noted for their educational achievement, trading activity, entrepreneurial skills, and arts and crafts work, particularly wood carving. Many are part of larger ethnic networks extending into several countries, which link West African states in the area. The colonial history of Sierra Leone was not placid. The indigenous people mounted several unsuccessful revolts against British rule and Creole domination. Most of the 20th century history of the colony was peaceful, however, and independence was achieved without violence.

Sierra Leone is an interesting country because it has no serious ethnic divisions. It has no serious religious divisions. It has no serious class divisions or regional divisions. People married across tribal boundaries, across religious boundaries, because the country is essentially a Muslim country with some Christians and some animists. But those divisions never really became an issue in early Sierra Leone. All ethnic groups use Krio as a second language, there is little ethnic segregation in urban areas. The two largest ethnic groups are the Temne in the northern part of the country and the Mende in the southern part; each of these groups is estimated to make up about 30 percent of the population.

Ethnic loyalty remained an important factor in government, the military, and business. Complaints of corruption within ethnic groups and ethnic discrimination in government appointments, contracts, military commissions, and promotions were common.

There did not appear to be a strong correspondence between ethnic or regional and political cleavages. Ethnic differences also did not appear to contribute appreciably to the Revolutionary United Front (RUF) rebellion, the 1997 coup, or the civil conflict. There was no identifiable ethnic or regional base of voluntary popular support for the rebels, who controlled territory by terror and coercion rather than by popular consent.

In October 1990, President Joseph Saidu Momoh set up a constitutional review commission to review the one-party 1978 constitution with a view to broadening the existing political process and strengthening and consolidating the democratic foundation and structure of the nation. There was great suspicion that Momoh was not serious, however, and All Peoples Congress (APC) rule was increasingly marked by abuses of power. The rebel war in the eastern part of the county posed an increasing burden on the country, and on April 29, 1992, a group of young Republic of Sierra Leone Military Forces (RSLMF) officers launched a military coup which sent Momoh into exile in Guinea and established the National Provisional Ruling Council (NPRC) as the ruling authority in Sierra Leone.

After 4 years of military government, which followed 25 years of one party rule, the Republic of Sierra Leone returned to civilian government after elections in March 1996. With 70 percent of the electorate participating, Alhaji Ahmad Tejan Kabbah was elected President in the first free and fair elections since 1967.

On 30 November 1996, President Kabbah signed the Abidjan Peace Agreement with the Revolutionary United Front (RUF), which had been attempting to overthrow successive governments since March 1991. Joint Government and RUF committees were to oversee disarmament and demobilization of RUF and government forces.

The RSLMF was supported by Nigerian and Guinean military contingents and by personnel working under a training and logistics contract with Executive Outcomes, a private South African mercenary firm. In compliance with the November 1996 Abidjan Peace Agreement, President Kabbah terminated the contract with Executive Outcomes at the end of January 1997. For 20 months, Executive Outcomes had played the critical role in government efforts to protect major towns and diamond mining areas from RUF attacks. Groups of traditional hunters (including the Mende *Kamajohs*, Temne *Kapras*, and Koranko *Tamaboros*) organized as civil defense militias, with government support defended their chiefdoms from RUF attacks and RSLMF looting. Neither the RSLMF nor the civil defense militia were fully under government control.

Though the threat had significantly diminished by the time of the democratic elections in 1996, which brought President Kabbah to office, a number of serious problems remained, in particular, the Revolutionary United Front (RUF) had refused to participate in the elections and continued to control some of Sierra Leone's territory. It turned out near impossible to reconcile a government unfriendly army (who backed another candidate having already had to give up power) and the well-organised pro-government kamajors (the regional armed militia who had been trained by foreign mercenaries officially employed by a previous government to fight the RUF).

This friction culminated in an army-led coup in May 1997—the Armed Forces Revolutionary Council (AFRC)-, which invited the RUF to join government in the hope to gain wider recognition. This was to be the first coup in Africa that had been effectively boycotted by the UN.

On 25 May 1997, dissident junior officers of the Republic of Sierra Leone Military Forces (RSLMF) violently seized power from the 14-month-old democratically elected Government of President Ahmed Tejan Kabbah. The United Nations Security Council condemned the overthrow of the government and called upon the military junta to restore the elected Government unconditionally. Major Johnny Paul Koroma, awaiting trial on charges stemming from a September 1996 coup attempt, was freed from prison and named Chairman of the new Armed Forces Revolutionary Council (AFRC). The AFRC immediately suspended the Constitution, banned political parties and all public demonstrations and meetings, and announced that all legislation would be made by military decree. Koroma invited the rebel Revolutionary United Front (RUF) to join the AFRC in exercising control over the country. The RUF quickly took control of the military junta, although Koroma remained nominal Chairman of the AFRC. The RUF had conducted an insurgency against successive governments.

After 25 May 1997, the RUF joined with RSLMF troops loyal to the AFRC junta and renamed itself the People's Army of Sierra Leone.

RSLMF forces loyal to the AFRC appear to function separately from RUF troops. They also fought occasional battles against each other. In June the AFRC formed joint military and police antilooting squads and gave them authority to shoot looters on sight.

On 08 October 1997, the United Nations Security Council imposed sanctions prohibiting the importation of weapons, military materiel, and petroleum as well as international travel by members of the military junta. Dozens of civilians were killed in clashes between AFRC/RUF forces and the ECOWAS Monitoring Group (ECOMOG) as ECOMOG attempted to enforce the sanctions. On 23 October 1997, AFRC/RUF and ECOWAS delegations signed a peace plan calling for the restoration to power of President Kabbah on April 22, 1998.

In January 1998, the coup was (only partly and only temporarily, it turned out) overturned by 'ECOMOG' forces (the Nigerian-lead West Africa multilateral peace-keeping force) and significant progress in restoring order was made, by the returning democratic government. Notably, this was the first time that a coup against a democratic government in Africa had been reversed without UN intervention, suggesting a new and positive level of regional co-operation.

In March 1998 the Government, led by President Ahmed Tejan Kabbah, who had been elected in 1996, was returned to power after 9 months in exile. The President's party, the Sierra Leone People's Party, has had a majority in the Parliament since 1996. The Government's return followed the February 1998 ouster of the Armed Forces Revolutionary Council and Revolutionary United Front. Throughout 1998 AFRC and RUF rebels committed numerous egregious abuses, including brutal killings, severe mutilations, and deliberate dismemberments, in a widespread campaign of terror against the civilian population known as "Operation No Living Thing."

One particularly vicious practice was cutting off the ears, noses, hands, arms, and legs of noncombatants who were unwilling to cooperate with or provide for the insurgents. The victims ranged from small children to elderly women; in some cases, one limb was cut off, in others two limbs, typically two hands or arms. Rebel forces also detained, decapitated, burned alive, and inflicted bullet and machete wounds on civilians; many died from their wounds before they could obtain any form of treatment. The rebel forces abducted missionaries and aid workers, ambushed humanitarian relief convoys and raided refugee sites. The junta forces continued the long-standing practice of abducting villagers and using them as forced laborers, as sex slaves, and as human shields during skirmishes with Government and ECOMOG forces. Boys were forced to become child soldiers. Rebel forces used rape as a terror tactic against women. Rebel atrocities prompted the internal displacement of hundreds of thousands of civilians.

The AFRC and RUF junta forces were defeated and driven out of Freetown by forces of the Economic Organization of West African States (ECOWAS) Monitoring Group (ECOMOG), led by the armed forces of Nigeria. In February and March 1998 there was fierce fighting throughout the country as ECOMOG and members of the Civil Defense Forces (CDF) continued to fight remnants of the AFRC and RUF, particularly in the larger cities outside the capital. However, government and ECOMOG forces failed to gain control of the whole country, and the civil conflict continued throughout 1998. In December 1998 AFRC AND RUF rebels infiltrated Freetown and, at year's end, controlled areas close to the capital.

Unfortunately clashes continued to occur between ECOMOG, rebel forces of the Revolutionary United Front (RUF), and the Armed Forces Revolutionary Council (AFRC) who attacked and re-entered Freetown in January, 1999. It was to be the saddest period of the 10year old conflict with reprisals and worst human suffering

Following the agreement of all parties to the principle of a negotiated settlement in February, 1999, a ceasefire was arranged for May 24, 1999 and a UN backed peace accord implemented.

The early months of 1999 were consumed with some of the bloodiest fighting in the country's eight-year civil war. By the end of January, the Nigerian-led ECOMOG peacekeeping force had regained control of Freetown—pushing the war back into Sierra Leone's rugged interior. But the cost of the assault on Freetown was staggering. Estimates suggest upwards of five or six-thousand people were killed, thousands more were injured, and still more thousands were left homeless by a rebel arson spree. The psychological impact of the invasion was equally important, leaving many Freetown residents—like Christina Leigh—fearing peace with the rebels would be impossible.

Pressure to resolve the crisis grew from the international community and from Nigeria's new civilian government, which wanted to bring its troops home. In May 1999 president Ahmad Tejan Kabbah allowed Foday Sankoh, the jailed chief of the Revolutionary United Front rebel movement to travel to Lome, Togo for talks with his military commanders. Eventually, teams of negotiators from the government and civilian groups joined the talks. After several weeks of difficult negotiations, a wide-ranging peace accord was signed on 07 July 1999.

Under the terms of the Lome accord, a cease-fire was agreed to, and the United Nations pledged to send a sizeable peacekeeping force to oversee the disarmament and demobilization of an estimated 45,000 combatants on both sides. Mr. Sankoh was pardoned and released from the death sentence he was facing for treason. Other combatants who had not engaged in heinous war crimes were also given a blanket amnesty, and the rebel factions were allotted four ministerial posts in a new government of national unity. Mr. Sankoh demanded and received a high-level position as well, being named chairman of a special commission on strategic resources—namely the diamonds that lie at the root of Sierra Leone's conflict.

In the months following the accord, Sierra Leone's peace process settled into the doldrums, and very little happened. Citing security concerns, Mr. Sankoh—and his ally former coup leader Johnny Paul Koromah—remained in Togo or Liberia, raising questions about their commitment to the July accord. Divisions also emerged between the two men—with Mr. Koromah's supporters accusing Mr. Sankoh of making their leader insignificant. And in September and October, a series of kidnappings and skirmishes erupted between the factions. Foday Sankoh returned to Sierra Leone in October, heralding what he called a new era, and asking the Sierra Leonean people for their forgiveness.

In the final weeks of 1999, Sierra Leone's peace process remained a work in progress, and many important parts of the July agreement had not been implemented. UN troops began arriving, but their numbers fell far short of the 6,000 authorized by the Security Council. This delay slowed the disarmament process, which had only recovered a token number of weapons, and raised suspicions on both sides. As Sierra Leone began the year 2000, disarmament was the key issue. Without it, political reforms, social reconciliation, jump starting the economy, and returning hundreds of thousands of refugees to their homes would be impossible.

In February 2000 the UN Security Council voted in enlarge UNAMSIL from 6,000 to 11,100 troops, making it the largest UN peacekeeping operation. At that time, the UN peacekeepers were taking on the duties of the departing 5,500-troop peacekeeping force of the Economic Community of West African States (ECOWAS), made up of units from Ghana, Guinea, Mali, and Nigeria.

All the parties to the settlement agreed to return to Freetown with a share in government and a UN peace keeping force, larger than that seen in Kosovo or Timor, was to be widely deployed in the country. However distrust continued to prevail on the intentions of each party, and UN peacekeepers after initial success in disarming RUF or AFRC groups, faced serious opposition when closing in on the alluvial diamond producing areas, and eventually fell victim to hostage taking in May 2000.

The Revolutionary United Front (RUF) subsequently reneged, refused to disarm and took hundreds of UN soldiers hostage. The United Nations force, which had been designed, equipped, and deployed as a peacekeeping force, was quickly forced into actual combat with RUF—one of the parties that had pledged to cooperate with it. After Mr. Sankoh's forces fought with UN peacekeepers and had taken hundreds of them hostage, he himself was taken into custody by the Sierra Leone government.

The UN in close cooperation with President Taylor of Liberia managed to liberate the hostages with limited casualties, and the RUF found itself without leadership after the capture and imprisonment of their discredited spokesman Foday Sankoh.

The UN Security Council on 19 May 2000 authorized the expansion of the UN Mission in Sierra Leone (UNAMSIL) to 13,000 troops and military observers. The expansion was approved when West African nations, especially Nigeria, offered additional troops to the beleaguered UNAMSIL after about 500 peacekeepers were detained by Revolutionary United Front (RUF) fighters who refused to be disarmed and the RUF began attacking UNAMSIL positions. In late May 2000 Secretary-General Kofi Annan recommended that the UN peacekeeping mission in Sierra Leone be increased to 16,500 in order to help stabilize the peace, and suggested that more troops might be needed in the future to solidify the peace process.

On 14 August 2000 the UN Security Council adopted Resolution 1315, which requested "the Secretary-General to negotiate an agreement with the Government of Sierra Leone to create an independent special court," whose subject matter jurisdiction "should include notably crimes against humanity, war crimes and other serious violations of international humanitarian law,"

The Special Court for Sierra Leone differs from the war crimes tribunals for the former Yugoslavia (ICTY) and Rwanda (ICTR). While the ICTY and ICTR were established by Chapter VII Resolutions of the Security Council, the Special Court is a treaty-based court established by the Agreement between the UN and Sierra Leone, and lacks the power of the ICTY and ICTR to assert primacy over national courts of other States or to order the surrender of an accused located in any other State. And unlike the ICTY and ICTR, which are composed exclusively of international judges elected by the UN General Assembly, and a Prosecutor selected by the Security Council, the Special Court is composed of both international and Sierra Leonean judges, prosecutors and staff. On 18 January 2002, the devastating 11-year civil conflict officially ended when all parties to the conflict issued a Declaration of the End of the War.

The Government since asserted control over the whole country, backed by a large U.N. peacekeeping force. Revolutionary United Front (RUF) insurgents, who fought successive governments since 1991, completed disarmament and demobilization. The Civil Defense Force (CDF), a government-allied militia, also disarmed and demobilized, but many

CDF members retained informal links to act in concert as a veterans' lobbying group and in their centuries-old role as members of traditional hunting societies. In May 2002 peaceful presidential and parliamentary elections were held; Ahmed Tejan Kabbah was re-elected President and his Sierra Leone People's Party (SLPP) won a large majority in Parliament.

Many international monitors declared the elections free and fair; however, there were numerous reports of election irregularities and abuses. Since the resumption of the disarmament, demobilization, and reintegration (DDR) process in May 2001, an estimated 72,500 former combatants disarmed; on 31 January 2002, the disarmament and demobilization sections of the program were completed. The process of reintegration continued at year's end.

The U.N. maintained a force of approximately 17,500 peacekeepers during most of the year. In September 2002 the U.N. Security Council decided to begin a gradual withdrawal of U.N. Mission to Sierra Leone (UNAMSIL) troops, to be completed by 2005. The official independent judiciary began functioning in areas abandoned during the war, but there still were sections of the country where the judiciary had not yet returned. The judiciary demonstrated substantial independence in practice but at times was subject to corruption.

The security situation in Sierra Leone, which has steadily improved since August 2000, was bolstered by the May 2002 re-election of President Ahmad Tejan Kabbah. However, areas near the Liberian border remain unstable as a result of continued border incursions by both the Armed Forces of Liberia (AFL) and LURD. According to UN OCHA, the humanitarian community operating in Sierra Leone has developed an alert system to inform agencies of security incidents near the border. On July 16, 2002, LURD militia abducted 20 people from the villages of Sanga, Kolu, and Manduvuluhun. The villagers were still reported missing at the end of August and are presumed to be in Liberia.

On September 5, 2002, U.N. Secretary General Kofi Annan recommended a six-month extension for the United Nations Mission in Sierra Leone (UNAMSIL) and the gradual downsizing of the mission from the current level of 17,000 peacekeeping troops to 5,000 by 2004. The U.N. Security Council approved the renewal of UNAMSIL's mandate on September 18. President Kabbah requested the extension in August 2002, citing the threat posed to Sierra Leone's fragile peace by renewed insecurity in Liberia.

The Disarmament, Demobilization, and Reintegration (DDR) campaign in Sierra Leone officially ended on January 7, 2002. According to the National Committee for Disarmament, Demobilization and Reintegration (NCDDR), approximately 21,000 of the 54,000 ex-combatants are participating in reintegration programs; 10,509 former soldiers have completed the program.

According to the U.N. Department of Peacekeeping Operations (UN DPKO), less than 12,000 IDPs remained in Sierra Leone as of July 2002. The remaining IDPs are mainly in the Tonkolili District. UNHCR completed the resettlement of registered Sierra Leonean IDPs from camps in the Pujehun District in August 2002 leaving the camps occupied almost exclusively by Liberian refugees. The Government of Sierra Leone (GOSL) expects resettlement efforts to be completed by October 2002.

The number of refugees returning to Sierra Leone from Liberia continues to decline. As of September 2002, UNHCR reports indicated that approximately 30,000 Sierra Leoneans remained in Liberia. According to UN OCHA, the refugees are awaiting more favourable social and economic conditions to develop in Sierra Leone before returning. In September, repatriation vessels, with capacities of 300, transported between 50 and 100 returnees per trip. On September 10, UNHCR announced the temporary suspension of repatriation efforts until refugee demand increases. According to UNHCR, of the 2,000 Sierra Leonean refugees in Nigeria, only 270 have registered for repatriation. UNHCR resumed overland repatriation of refugees from Guinea following a 42-day suspension resulting from logistical problems. As of August 2002, 42,000 Sierra Leonean refugees remained in Guinea.

Focus has since been on retraining a new Sierra Leone army, as well as further Ecomog reinforcement troops in Nigeria, by the UK and USA respectively. Meanwhile strategies have gradually been put in place to reduce illicit 'conflict' diamonds exports in order to reduce the RUF's source of funding. It is expected that an enlarged UN/Ecomog/ Coordinated S L army possibly incorporating previous kamajors would eventually defeat the RUF and remaining AFRC now calling themselves the 'West Side Boys' illfamed for their capture of strayed British soldiers in Summer 2000; however a new RUF leadership under pressure seems more anxious to push for a negotiated settlement, as long as they can overcome their view that the UK's involvement is an extension of mercenary deployment that successfully crushed them years earlier.

High level visits demonstrate the world's readiness to alleviate the human tragedy and bring lasting peace to the subregion. Throughout the 10 year period, Sierra Leone has constantly improved its minerals legislation. For the time being a situation of force majeure exists, with the suspension of exploration work on Mano's licences. It is hoped that preliminary visits to permit areas in Sierra Leone will be possible in the near future.

Sierra Leone is rich in minerals and is one of the world's most important sources of large diamonds. The country also hosts gold, platinum, rutile, chrome, bauxite and iron. Major producers have included the Nord/Consolidated Rutile world-class rutile deposit, Alusuisse's bauxite operations and the famous Kono diamond fields worked for many years by Selection Trust at Yengema and Koidu.

CHAPTER SIX

The Peace-Deal Election and Transfer of Power for Peace Maintenance

The three stages of conflict resolution for a peace deal

<u>What is a conflict?</u>

A conflict is a dispute that occurs between two parties emanating from misunderstanding or disagreement over an issue or a deal. This situation is usually common and it happens between couples (husband and wife), brothers and sisters of the same family, in government, different political parties, etc. As conflict is therefore a feeling that results into accusing one party by the other party, of inflicting what they do not like or being treated unfairly, against the law, the dispute might result into quarrelling, fighting, tribalism, racism, segregation, civil war, international war, etc. Once a conflict start, it develops to different stages and the consequence could be devastating costing lives, properties or even lives that may include the innocent, the poor, the rich, women, children, and the powerful in high places. We have all witnessed conflict and the result unfolded in Libya which resulted into costing "the head of state" his life, including some members of his family and many other citizens. My personal advice to my readers is that: "don't encourage conflict to start and carry on in any relationship".

Of course, Sierra Leoneans have once experienced conflicts (arm conflict) perpetrated by my brother, Foday Sankoh and his Revolutionary United Front (RUF). According to my brother, Foday

Sankoh, he was not pleased the mannerism in which Siaka Stevens and the All Peoples Congress (APC) mismanaged the wealth of Sierra Leone and for many years he went on studying and developing strategies to bring the situation to the attention of the nation and his research discovered that the only way that everybody was to take him serious was through rebel-group formation to put across their demand on behalf of the country that would halt APC as a ruling force.

Although Siaka Stevens was already dead by then, Joseph Siadu Momoh, who was his predecessor, the APC leader and head of state of Sierra Leone cowered and flew into neighbouring Guinea, when junior army officers from the civil war front, arrived at state house to solicit for funding to buy foods and medicines and this motivated the junta regime headed by young Valentine E M Strasser.

First stage of conflict resolution: Once a conflict start, it develops to different stages and the devastating effects could be catastrophic resulting into divorce as far as wars, etc. My personal advice to my readers, as I said earlier on, is that: **"don't encourage conflict to start and carry on in any relationship".**

Although this is sometimes unavoidable in our relationships, especially when one party feels advantaged of the disadvantage suffered by the other.

The first step to conflict resolution is to **accept that there is an unacceptable condition** and it should be straightened for the benefits of all. Accept your own part of the blame and take every responsibility genuinely.

Second stage-Peace process: At this stage, all parties will be ready to negotiate to enhance the conflict resolution. This stage is the most painful because during this time, all parties are required to give up most of what they valued as being precious to satisfy the other party in order that both remain happy and live together without disturbance from any party, ever after. What they give up most is the peace deal.

The third stage-Peace maintenance: This stage is usually the most fragile of the conflict resolution process. At this stage, the parties involved in the peace process and affected by the conflict will reflect on how well they acted and what benefits they got from the resolution or peace process. It is therefore fragile because any party can feel that they have been tricked and led into agreeing into signing a deal that is not in their own interest and that the deal is not fair on them. Such pressures may cause the negotiation leaders to break the peace deal and start the conflict all over again.

The peace deal therefore continues during the peace maintenance period in order to give chance to the peace to hold up. How was this handled in Sierra Leone peace process and what were the peace deals?

CHAPTER SEVEN

Tajan Kabbah's role

Whether anybody likes it or not, SLPP's Tejan Kabbah is the most strategic president Sierra Leone has ever had in the history of politics of that country. He assumed presidential power to perform the most important task the country ever needed at the right time, for the right purpose; in the middle of civil war, when there as no time for him to enjoy presidential "sweet of office" and subsequently further, his wife Patricia Kabbah (may her soul rest in peace) died.

When that wound was just very fresh in the minds of the state, it was the time when the All Peoples Congress (APC) supporters went into their jubilation of singing in the streets of Freetown with their new invention of provocation "Tejan Kabbah na Koboko" meaning that Tejan Kabbah has no wife. May I take this moment, in my capacity as a genuine Sierra Leonean, to please apologise to Tejan Kabbah and express my personal disgust for such a shameful display of unacceptable behaviour, because that is not Sierra Leonean style in any capacity, wherever. Tejan Kabbah's term of office will ever be remembered as the term of "peace search era" in Sierra Leone.

He embarked immediately on peace search mission by visiting Foday Sankoh and the RUF in the bush to discuss how best they can come to terms leading to cessation of conflict in the country, as he accepted that there was a problem.

I came to learn the practical theory from Sierra Leone experience that peace negotiation in theory, always requires giving up some benefits to your opponent and sometimes the peace deal cost very dearly but beneficial as long as the peace deal comes to fruition. Also, a peace deal, as in Sierra Leone's case starts with such sacrifices, and continues during and **after the peace negotiation, to maintain the peace process**. Tejan Kabbah had to come to terms with my brother, Foday Sankoh to the extent of appointing that rebel leader as the vice president of Sierra Leone in charge of all mineral resources in the country including diamonds, the nation's source of wealth.

As a result, some very strong SLPP party supporters who did not understand the strategy found Tejan Kabbah disgusting, unacceptable and difficult to work with; fell out with him and eventually left the party and some even switched over to other parties while others started their own political party and collided with other parties to undermine SLPP strongholds.

Another major problem Tejan Kabbah had with SLPP supporters was that he was never frequent in the party office, but his excuse was that he was not a president for SLPP but a president of Sierra Leone, the nation and therefore his office of frequency was the state house office, where he deals with state affairs.

Therefore, the APC's victory of 2007 that took Ernest Koroma to state house was still part of the peace deal agreement (**peace maintenance-after peace deal**) of Sierra Leone negotiated by Tejan Kabbah; although to great shock of Solomon Berewa with the APC as they have raised high level of threats for starting the war all over again because the RUF overthrew their democratically elected government for which Joseph Saidu Momoh was the leader.

That has worked well for the country and thank God for bringing strategic Tejan Kabbah at that crucial time and to use him well for the benefits of all in Sierra Leone.

CHAPTER EIGHT

The Trial & Prosecution of Charles Taylor

The Sierra Leone civil war came about as a result of spill over effects from the Liberia civil war collaborated together with my brother, Foday Sankoh of RUF and the then head of State of Liberia, Charles Taylor.

One of the local problems in African countries is boarder controls among countries. In Sierra Leone—Liberia situation, people of both nations have trading with each other in different categories for a very long time to the extend that movement of people from eastern part of Sierra Leone into the Western part of Liberia ahs been borderless. It has since been a common practice for Sierra Leoneans to farm in Liberia while living in Sierra and verse versa. In Liberia, there are many Mende and Kissy tribal people as well as Gola people who are Liberians in national identity.

SPECIAL COURT FOR SIERRA LEONE

TRIAL CHAMBER II

Before: Justice Richard Lussick, Presiding Judge

Justice Teresa Doherty

Justice Julia Sebutinde

Justice El Hadji Malick Sow, Alternate Judge

Registrar: Binta Mansaray

Case No.: SCSL-03-1-T

Date: 26 April 2011

PROSECUTOR v.

Charles Ghankay TAYLOR

JUDGEMENT SUMMARY

Office of the Prosecutor: Defence Counsel for Charles G. Taylor:

Brenda J. Hollis

Nicholas Koumjian

Mohamed Bangura

Kathryn Howarth

Leigh Lawrie

Ruth Mary Hackler

Ula Nathai-Lutchman

Nathan Quick

Maja Dimitrova

James Pace

Courtenay Griffiths, Q.C.

Terry Munyard

Morris Anyah

Silas Chekera

James Supuwood

Logan Hambrick2

SUMMARY JUDGEMENT

PROSECUTOR V. CHARLES GHANKAY TAYLOR

1. Trial Chamber II, composed of Justice Richard Lussick, presiding, Justice Teresa Doherty, Justice Julia Sebutinde, with alternate judge Justice El Hadji Malick Sow, today delivers its Judgement in the case of the Prosecutor v. Charles Ghankay Taylor. For the purposes of this hearing, the Chamber will briefly summarise its findings. This is a summary only. The written Judgement, which is the only authoritative version, will be made available subsequently.

Introduction

2. Charles Ghankay Taylor was elected President of Liberia and took office on 2 August 1997. On 4 June 2003, his Indictment by the Special Court and Warrant of Arrest were unsealed, and on 11 August 2003 he stepped down from the Presidency and went into exile in Nigeria. In 2003, the Accused applied to the Special Court to quash his Indictment and set aside the warrant for his arrest on the grounds that he was immune from any exercise of the jurisdiction of this Court by virtue of the fact that at the time the Indictment and Warrant of Arrest were issued he was a sitting Head of State.

This application was denied by the Trial Chamber, and its decision was upheld by the Appeals Chamber on 31 May 2004, on the ground that the sovereign equality of states does not prevent a Head of State from being prosecuted before an international criminal tribunal or court. Accordingly, the Appeals Chamber held that the official position of Charles Taylor as an incumbent Head of State at the time when these criminal proceedings were initiated against him was not a bar to his prosecution by this Court.

On 29 March 2006, the Accused was arrested in Nigeria by Nigerian authorities, following a request by Liberian President Johnson-Sirleaf that he be surrendered to the Special Court pursuant to the Warrant of Arrest. Shortly thereafter he was transferred into the custody of the Special Court in Freetown, Sierra Leone, and was formally arraigned on 3 April 2006, when he pleaded not guilty to all counts in the Indictment. Because of security concerns, the Accused was transferred to The Hague on 20 June 2006.

3. The armed conflict in Sierra Leone started in March 1991 when armed fighters known as the Revolutionary United Front (RUF), led by Foday Sankoh, attacked Sierra Leone from Liberia. The RUF continued their insurgency against the Government despite the Abidjan Peace Accord in November 1996. In a coup on 25 May 1997, members of the Sierra Leone Army overthrew the democratically elected Government of Ahmad Tejan Kabbah and invited the RUF to join its Junta Government, called the Armed Forces Revolutionary Council (AFRC).

4. As leader of the NPFL (National Patriotic Front of Liberia) and later as President of Liberia, the Accused is alleged to have acted in concert with members of the RUF (Revolutionary United Front), AFRC (Armed Forces Revolutionary Council),

AFRC/RUF Junta or alliance and/or Liberian fighters, including members and exmembers of the NPFL (Liberian fighters). Specifically, in that capacity, the Accused is alleged to have assisted, encouraged, directed and/or controlled the above mentioned warring factions in conducting armed attacks in the territory of Sierra Leone from 30 November 1996 to 18 January 2002 (the Indictment period). The attacks included terrorizing the civilian population including burning of civilian homes, murder, sexual violence, physical violence, illegal recruitment of child soldiers, abduction and forced labour, and looting.

Procedural Background

5. The Prosecution case commenced on 4 June 2007 and closed on 27 February

2009. During the Defence case, the Prosecution was granted leave to re-open its case to call three additional witnesses who testified on 5, 9 and 10 August 2010. In sum, 94 witnesses testified for the Prosecution, including three expert witnesses. A total of 782 Prosecution exhibits were admitted into evidence including five expert reports.

6. The Defence opened its case on 13 July 2009 and closed on 12 November 2010, having called 21 witnesses, including the Accused, who testified for seven months, from 14 July 2009 until 18 February 2010. A total of 740 Defence exhibits were admitted into evidence. 4

7. Prosecution closing arguments were heard on 8 and 9 February 2011. Defence closing arguments were heard on 9 and 10 March 2011. Oral responses by both parties were heard on 11 March 2011.

8. After 420 trial days over the course of three years and ten months, the case was formally closed on 11 March 2011. A total of 115

witnesses testified, 1,522 exhibits were admitted into evidence, 49,622 pages of trial records were transcribed and 281 written interlocutory decisions were issued by the Trial Chamber.

Summary of the Charges

9. The Accused is charged with 11 Counts under the Indictment. Five of these counts charge the Accused with crimes against humanity punishable under Article 2 of the Statute, in particular: murder (Count 2), rape (Count 4), sexual slavery (Count 5), other inhumane acts (Count 8) and enslavement (Count 10). Five additional counts charge the Accused with violations of Article 3 Common to the Geneva Conventions and of Additional Protocol II, punishable under Article 3 of the Statute, in particular: acts of terrorism (Count 1), violence to life, health and physical or mental well-being of persons, in particular murder (Count 3); outrages upon personal dignity (Count 6); violence to life, health and physical or mental well-being of persons, in particular cruel treatment (Count 7); and pillage (Count 11).

The remaining count charges the Accused with conscripting or enlisting children under the age of 15 years into armed forces or groups, or using them to participate actively in hostilities (Count 9), a serious violation of international humanitarian law punishable under Article 4 of the Statute. 10. The Indictment charges that the Accused is individually criminally responsible, under Article 6(1) and 6(3) of the Statute, for the crimes referred to above.

11. The Accused pleaded not guilty to each of the counts charged in the Indictment. Summary of the Defence Case12. The Defence accepts that crimes against humanity and war crimes were committed during the Indictment period in the course of the armed conflict in Sierra Leone, but denies that the Accused is responsible. The Defence submits that the burden of proof is upon the Prosecution to prove beyond reasonable

doubt (i) that the crimes were actually committed; (ii) that the crimes fulfil all the legal elements of Articles 2, 3 and 4 of the Statute; and (iii) that there is a nexus between the alleged crimes and the Accused.

13. As part of its case, the Defence maintained that the Accused, through his Diplomatic efforts, played a substantial role in fostering peace and security in Sierra Leone, that his contribution to the peace process was significant, and that his prosecution has from the outset been "selective and vindictive in nature . . . on the basis of political motives and interests." The Defence also challenged the credibility of the Prosecution evidence.

The Trial Chamber has considered a number of preliminary issues in its written Judgement, including the issue of selective prosecution and a number of fair trial issues raised by the Defence. With regard to the issue of selective prosecution, the Trial Chamber finds that the Accused was not singled out for selective prosecution. Summary of Findings on Crimes Committed

14. The Trial Chamber finds that the Chapeau Requirements in respect of the crimes against humanity, violations of article 3 common to the Geneva Conventions and of Additional Protocol II and other serious violations of international humanitarian law charged in the Indictment, have been proved by the Prosecution beyond reasonable doubt.

15. The Trial Chamber has examined the evidence presented in relation to the crimes that members of the RUF, AFRC, the AFRC/RUF Junta or alliance, and/or Liberian fighters allegedly committed in Sierra Leone between 30 November 1996 and about 18 January 2002. The Trial Chamber finds that the crimes charged in Counts 1 to 11 were committed. The findings on each of these crimes will be summarized in turn. 6 MURDER, a Crime Against Humanity, punishable under Article 2.a. of the Statute. (Count 2) and/or VIOLENCE to Life, Health

and Physical or Mental Well-Being of Persons, in particular MURDER, a Violation of Article 3 Common to the Geneva Conventions and of Additional Protocol II, punishable under Article 3.a. of the Statute (Count 3)

16. The Trial Chamber finds that the Prosecution has proved beyond reasonable doubt that members of the RUF, AFRC, AFRC/RUF Junta or alliance, and/or Liberian fighters, murdered civilians in various locations in the following districts of Sierra Leone:

17. In Kenema District between about 25 May 1997 and about 31 March 1998.

18. In Kono District between about 1 February 1998 and about 31 January 2000.

19. In Freetown and the Western Area between about 21 December 1998 and 28

February 1999.

20. In Kailahun District between about 1 February 1998 and about 30 June 1998.

RAPE, a Crime Against Humanity, punishable under Article 2.g. of the Statute

(Count 4)

21. The Trial Chamber finds that the Prosecution has proved beyond reasonable doubt that members of the RUF, AFRC, AFRC/RUF Junta or alliance, and Liberian fighters committed widespread acts of rape

against women and girls in various locations in the following districts of Sierra Leone:

22. In Kono District between about 1 February and about 31 December 1998.

23. In Freetown and the Western Area between about 21 December 1998 and about 28 February 1999. 7

24. In Kailahun District in 1998 and 1999 women and girls were raped in various locations which were not charged in the Indictment. The Trial Chamber makes no finding of guilt for these crimes for reasons fully set out in the written judgement.

SEXUAL SLAVERY, a Crime Against Humanity, punishable under Article 2.g. of the Statute (Count 5)

25. The Trial Chamber finds that the Prosecution has proved beyond reasonable doubt that between about 30 November 1996 and about 18 January 2002, members of the RUF, AFRC, AFRC/RUF Junta or alliance and Liberian fighters committed widespread acts of sexual slavery against civilian women and girls in Sierra Leone in various locations in the following districts of Sierra Leone:

26. In Kono District between about 1 February 1998 and about 31 December 1998.

27. In Kailahun District in 1998 and 1999.

28. In Freetown and the Western Area between about 21 December 1998 and about 28 February 1999.

OUTRAGES UPON PERSONAL DIGNITY, a Violation of Article 3 Common to the Geneva Conventions and of Additional Protocol II, punishable under Article 3.e. of the Statute (Count 6).

29. The Trial Chamber finds that the Prosecution has proved beyond reasonable doubt that members of the RUF, AFRC, AFRC/RUF Junta or alliance and Liberian fighters committed widespread acts of outrages upon the personal dignity of civilian women and girls by acts such as forcing them to undress in public and by raping them and committing other acts of sexual abuse sometimes in full view of the public, and in full view of family members, in various locations in the following districts of Sierra Leone: 8

30. In Kono District between about 1 February 1998 and about 31 December 1998;

31. In Freetown and the Western Area between about 21 December 1998 and about 28 February 1999;

32. In Kailahun District in 1998 and 1999 outrages upon personal dignity were committed against women and girls in various locations not charged in the Indictment. The Trial Chamber makes no finding of guilt for these crimes for reasons fully set out in the written judgement.

VIOLENCE to life, health and physical or mental well-being of persons, in particularCRUEL TREATMENT, a Violation of Article 3 Common to the Geneva Conventions and of Additional Protocol II, punishable under Article 3.a. of the Statute (Count 7); and/or OTHER INHUMANE ACTS, a Crime Against Humanity, punishable under Article 2.i. of the Statute (Count 8)

33. The Trial Chamber finds that the Prosecution has proved beyond reasonable doubt that members of the RUF, AFRC, AFRC/RUF Junta or alliance, and Liberian fighters committed widespread acts of physical violence against civilians in various locations in the following districts of Sierra Leone:

34. In Kono District between about 1 February 1998 and about 31 December 1998, civilians were forced to endure cruel treatment including having words carved into their bodies, and amputations of limbs.

35. In Kailahun District, crimes of physical violence were committed not charged in the Indictment. The Trial Chamber makes no findings of guilt for these crimes for reasons fully set out in the written judgement.

36. In Freetown and the Western Area between about 21 December 1998 and about 28 February 1999 civilians were subjected to cruel treatment, including the amputations of limbs.9 CONSCRIPTING OR ENLISTING CHILD SOLDIERS INTO THE ARMED FORCES OR USING THEM IN HOSTILITIES, and Other Serious Violations of International Humanitarian Law, punishable under Article 4.c. of the Statute (Count 9)

37. The Trial Chamber finds that the Prosecution has proved beyond reasonable doubt that between about 30 November 1996 and about 18 January 2002, members of the RUF, AFRC, AFRC/RUF Junta or alliance and Liberian fighters conscripted and enlisted children under the age of 15 into their armed groups and used them to participate actively in the hostilities in the following districts of Sierra Leone:

38. In Tonkolili District, children under the age of 15 were abducted and conscripted into the RUF at Kangari Hills from early 1996 until

May 1997. Between 500 and 1000 children had "RUF" carved into their forehead or back to prevent escape.

39. In Kailahun District, children under the age of 15 were conscripted into the RUF throughout 1998 and 1999, and underwent military training at Bunumbu training base, also known as "Camp Lion", and at Buedu Field.

40. In Kono District during the Indictment period, children under the age of 15 were conscripted into the RUF and AFRC at various locations and were used to participate actively in hostilities and to amputate limbs, guard diamond mines, go on food-finding missions, as bodyguards, to man checkpoints and in armed combat.

41. In Bombali District, children under the age of 15 were conscripted into the RUF and AFRC between 1998 and 2000, underwent military training at various locations and participated actively in hostilities.

42. In Port Loko District between January 1999 and April/May 1999, a child under the age of 15 was abducted, conscripted into the AFRC and used for active participation in hostilities in Masiaka.

43. In Kenema District during the Junta period, children under the age of 15 were used as armed guards for mining sites. 10

44. In Koinadugu District between March and May 1998, children under the age of 15 were used to participate actively in hostilities and at least one child under the age of 15 was used to fight against the Kamajors.

45. In Freetown and the Western Area, children under the age of 15 were used to participate actively in hostilities in Benguema from the end of January until March 1999 and during the Freetown attack

in January 1999. ENSLAVEMENT, a Crime Against Humanity, punishable under Article 2.c. of the Statute (Count 10)

46. The Trial Chamber finds that the Prosecution has proved beyond reasonable doubt that between 30 November 1996 and about 18 January 2002, members of the RUF, AFRC, AFRC/RUF Junta or alliance and Liberian fighters intentionally exercised powers of ownership over civilians by depriving them of their freedom and forcing them to work, thus committing the crime of enslavement in various locations in the following districts of Sierra Leone:

47. In Kenema District between about 1 July 1997 and about 28 February 1998, civilians were abducted and forced to mine for diamonds.

48. In Kono District throughout 1998 and 1999, civilians were abducted and used as forced labour to carry loads, perform domestic chores, go on food-finding missions, undergo military training, and work in diamond mines.

49. In Kailahun District between 30 November 1996 and July 2000 civilians were abducted and used as forced labour to carry loads, collect arms and ammunition, construct the Buedu airstrip, undergo military training, farm, fish, perform domestic chores and go on food-finding missions.

50. In Freetown and the Western Area between about 21 December 1998 and about 28 February 1999, civilians were abducted and used as forced labour to carry loads, perform domestic chores and destroy a bridge. 11 PILLAGE, a Violation of Article 3 Common to the Geneva Conventions and of Additional Protocol II, punishable under Article 3.f. of the Statute (Count 11)

51. The Trial Chamber finds that the Prosecution has proved beyond reasonable doubt that members of the RUF, AFRC, AFRC/RUF Junta or alliance, and Liberian fighters, engaged in widespread and unlawful taking of civilian property in various locations in the following districts of Sierra Leone:

52. In Kono District, between about 1 February 1998 and about 31 December 1998, civilian goods were looted, money and diamonds were looted from a bank and, as part of 'Operation Pay Yourself', civilian homes and shops were looted.

53. In Bombali District, numerous instances of looting of civilian property occurred between 1 February 1998 and 30 April 1998. Money from a bank was also looted.

54. In Port Loko District between 1 February 1998 and 30 April 1998 there were numerous instances of looting of civilian property as part of Operation Pay Yourself.

55. In Freetown and the Western Area between about 21 December 1998 and about 28 February 1999, widespread looting of civilian property from residences and businesses occurred.

ACTS OF TERRORISM, a Violation of Article 3 Common to the Geneva

Conventions and of Additional Protocol II, punishable under Article 3.d. of the Statute (Count 1)

56. The Trial Chamber finds that the Prosecution has proved beyond reasonable doubt that members of the RUF, AFRC, AFRC/RUF Junta or alliance, and Liberian fighters committed acts of terrorism by

committing the crimes described in counts 2 to 8 as part of a campaign to terrorize the civilian population of Sierra Leone.

57. There was evidence in the crimes described in counts 2 to 8 of public executions and amputations; people were beheaded and their heads displayed at checkpoints; during 12 "Operation No Living Thing," during the Junta Period in Kenema Town, a civilian was killed in full public view and then his body was disembowelled and his intestines stretched across the road to make a "checkpoint"; women and girls were raped in public; people were burned alive in their homes. The Trial Chamber finds beyond reasonable doubt that the purpose of these atrocities charged in counts 2 to 8 was to instil terror in the civilian population.

58. However, some acts of violence, even when committed in a campaign whose primary purpose was to terrorise the civilian population, may not have been committed in furtherance of such a campaign. The Trial Chamber finds that this is the case with the acts of violence underlying the crimes of Child Soldiers (Count 9), Enslavement (Count 10), and Pillage (Count 11). The Trial Chamber therefore finds that the crime of acts of terrorism has not been established for these counts.

59. The Trial Chamber also finds that the Prosecution has proved beyond reasonable doubt that acts of terrorism were committed by the widespread burning of civilian property with the primary purpose of terrorizing the civilian population in various locations in Kono District between about 1 February 1998 and about 31 December 1998, and in various locations in Freetown and Western Area between about 21 December 1998 and February 1999.Summary of Findings on the Role of the Accused.

60. The Trial Chamber will now summarize its factual findings on the role of the Accused.

The Role of the Accused before 1996.

61. The Trial Chamber has considered evidence prior to the Indictment period only for the purposes of clarifying the context, or establishing by inference the elements of criminal conduct that occurred during the material period, or demonstrating a consistent pattern of conduct. 13

62. Evidence before the Trial Chamber establishes the following. At the end of the 1980s, a number of West African revolutionaries were trained in Libya, including Charles Taylor from Liberia, Ali Kabbah and Foday Sankoh from Sierra Leone and Kukoi Samba Sanyang (a.k.a. Dr. Manneh) from the Gambia. The Accused met Sankoh in Libya, although the exact circumstances of their meeting are not known. Contrary to the Prosecution's submissions, the evidence did not establish that prior to 1996, Taylor, Sankoh and Dr. Manneh participated in any common plan involving the crimes alleged in the Indictment, nor in fact, that the three men even met together. Furthermore, the evidence was that during the pre-indictment period Sankoh operated independently of the

Accused, and that while he relied at times on Taylor's guidance and support, Sankoh did not take orders from the Accused.

63. During the pre-Indictment period the Accused provided the RUF with a training camp in Liberia, instructors, recruits and material support, including food and other supplies. However, again contrary to the Prosecution's submissions, the evidence did not establish that the RUF were under the superior authority of the Accused or the NPFL chain of command, or that they were instructed in NPFL terror tactics.

64. The Accused supported the invasion of Sierra Leone in March 1991. NPFL troops actively participated in the invasion, but the Prosecution failed to prove that the Accused participated in the planning of the invasion. The Prosecution also failed to prove that the support of the Accused for the invasion of Sierra Leone was undertaken pursuant to a common purpose to terrorize the civilian population of Sierra Leone. Rather, the evidence shows that the Accused and Sankoh had a common interest in fighting common enemies, namely ULIMO, a Liberian insurgency group in Sierra Leone, and the Sierra Leonean Government forces, which supported ULIMO.

65. The Accused withdrew his NPFL troops from Sierra Leone after the fallout between NPFL and RUF troops in 1992, culminating in Operations Top 20, Top 40, and Top Final. While the Defence maintains that the Accused had no further contact or cooperation with Sankoh, the leader of the RUF, after 1992 following Top Final, the Trial Chamber finds otherwise. Although the Liberia-Sierra Leone border was 'closed' by 14 ULIMO and the Sierra Leone government forces, it remained porous, enabling the flow of arms, ammunition and other supplies from Liberia into Sierra Leone during the remainder of the pre-Indictment period. For example, there was evidence that the Accused provided arms and ammunition to Sankoh for an attack on Kono in November 1992, and he advised Sankoh prior to and following the attack on Sierra Rutile. The Accused also asked Sankoh to send troops in 1993 to help him fight ULIMO. The Role of the Accused during the Indictment Period

Military Operations 66.

In February 1998, ECOMOG forces intervened in Sierra Leone and expelled the RUF/AFRC Junta from Freetown, reinstating Tejan Kabbah's SLPP Government to power in March 1998. Although ECOMOG initially forced RUF and AFRC forces to withdraw from

Kono, under the orders of AFRC leader Johnny Paul Koroma, these forces managed to recapture Koidu Town in late February-early March 1998. A few weeks later, ECOMOG forces regained control of Koidu Town. In mid-June 1998, forces under the ultimate direction of Sam Bockarie, who had by then assumed leadership of the renegade RUF/AFRC Junta forces, made another attempt to re-take Koidu Town, codenamed Operation Fitti-Fatta. The Fitti-Fatta attack was unsuccessful, and in late November-early December 1998, after a trip by Bockarie to Liberia where he met with the Accused, a meeting was held at Waterworks in which Bockarie ordered RUF/AFRC troops under his command to carry out a two pronged attack on Kono and Kenema, with Freetown as the ultimate target. The attacks on Kenema and Kono were launched in midDecember 1998. While the former was unsuccessful, the latter attack succeeded, and the RUF/AFRC troops continued towards Freetown. On 6 January 1999, a group of predominantly AFRC troops led by Alex Tamba Brima (a.k.a. Gullit) launched an assault on Freetown.

67. The Trial Chamber will now summarize its findings on the assistance provided by the Accused in these military operations.

68. From the time of the ECOMOG Intervention, the Accused and his subordinates communicated to the AFRC/RUF forces the imperative to maintain control over Kono, a 15diamondiferous area. When the AFRC/RUF forces were pulling out of Kono during the Intervention, the radio station of Benjamin Yeaten, Director of the Accused's Special Security Service, intercepted a radio transmission between AFRC/RUF radio stations about the withdrawal and intervened to ask why the forces were withdrawing. Then, in several satellite phone conversations with Johnny Paul Koroma, who was trying to make arrangements to get to Liberia by helicopter, the Accused told Koroma to capture Kono. After a first failed attempt, the Accused gave instructions for a second attack, which led to the ultimate recapture of Koidu Town in

Kono District in late February-early March 1998. Once Kono had been recaptured, the Accused told Bockarie to be sure to maintain control of Kono for the purpose of trading diamonds with him for arms and ammunition.

69. The Accused advised Bockarie to recapture Kono following its loss to ECOMOG, again so that the diamonds there could be used to purchase arms and ammunition. Such advice was transmitted to RUF commanders both through Bockarie and Liberian emissaries Daniel Tamba (a.k.a Jungle) and/or Ibrahim Bah and resulted in the Fitti-Fatta attack in mid-June 1998.

70. In addition to urging the RUF and AFRC to capture and hold Kono, the Accused supplied arms and ammunition for the operations in the Kono District in early 1998 and for Operation Fitti-Fatta.

71. In November/December 1998, when Bockarie met with the Accused in Monrovia, the Accused jointly designed with Bockarie the two-pronged attack on Kono, Kenema and Freetown outlined by Bockarie to his commanders in a meeting at Waterworks on his return to Sierra Leone. Although the idea to advance towards Freetown was already in discussion when Bockarie went to Monrovia, the Accused emphasised to Bockarie the need to first attack Kono District and told Bockarie to make the operation "fearful" in order to pressure the Government of Sierra Leone into negotiations on the release of Foday Sankoh from prison, as well as to use "all means" to get to Freetown. Subsequently, Bockarie named the operation "Operation No Living Thing," implying that anything that stood in their way should be eliminated. 16

72. At this time there were two plans to attack Freetown, one made by Bockarie with the Accused, and one made by breakaway AFRC commander Solomon Anthony Joseph Musa (a.k.a. SAJ Musa), whose troops had started an advance towards Freetown at the end of June/

beginning of July 1998. Consistent with his discussions with the Accused, Bockarie invited SAJ Musa after the Waterworks meeting to join his efforts to attack Freetown but Musa refused. However, with SAJ Musa's death in or around 23 December 1998, when Gullit took over the leadership of the troops at Benguema and resumed contact with Bockarie, Bockarie and Gullit coordinated in their efforts to capture Freetown. From that point onwards, SAJ Musa's original plan was abandoned, and Gullit followed the Bockarie/Taylor plan, as had been contemplated by Bockarie and the Accused. During the operation, Bockarie exercised effective command and control over Gullit, issuing a number of instructions to Gullit, including the order to use terror tactics against the civilian population on the retreat from Freetown. The Trial Chamber did not make a finding as to how SAJ Musa was killed, but noted that the possibility of his death had been mentioned by Bockarie at the time of the Waterworks meeting. 73. The Accused gave advice to Bockarie and received updates in relation to the progress of the operations in Kono and Freetown in the implementation of their plan. Bockarie was in frequent contact via radio or satellite phone with the Accused in December 1998 and January 1999, either directly or through Benjamin Yeaten. Yeaten also travelled to Sierra Leone to meet with Bockarie in Buedu during this period. However, it is not clear that the Accused had any level of control over the conduct of these operations. Of the instructions allegedly given to Bockarie by the Accused during this period, only one was proved beyond reasonable doubt, that being that the Accused instructed Bockarie to transfer some of the Pademba Road prisoners to Buedu. This finding is insufficient to establish, as the Prosecution has alleged, that the Accused directed or had control over the Kono and Freetown operations in December 1998 and January 1999.

74. In addition to planning and advising on the Kono-Freetown operation, the Accused also provided military and other support. He facilitated the purchase and transport of a large shipment of arms and

ammunition from Burkina Faso in around 17November 1998 which was used in the attacks on Kono and Kenema in December 1998, where further arms and ammunition were captured. These arms and ammunition were in turn sent to the troops in Freetown in January 1999 and also used by the RUF and AFRC in joint attacks on the outskirts of Freetown. The Accused also sent personnel in the form of at least four former Sierra Leone Army (SLA) fighters who participated in the attack on Kono, as well as 20 former NPFL fighters who were part of the forces under the command of Gullit that entered Freetown, and a group of 150 fighters with Abu Keita (a former ULIMO member), known as the Scorpion Unit, who participated in the attack on Kenema.

75. During the Freetown operation, the Accused's subordinates in Liberia also transmitted "448 messages" to RUF forces to warn them of impending ECOMOG jet attacks. These messages originated in both Sierra Leone and Liberia. Operational Support

76. In addition to support for specific military operations, the Accused provided to the RUF, and the RUF/AFRC alliance, communications support, financial support, military training, technical support and other operational support. Of these, communications support, facilitation and transport of materiel and personnel and the provision of a guesthouse to the RUF were sustained and significant.

77. Concerning communications assistance, following the invasion of Sierra Leone in 1991, the NPFL provided radio operators and equipment to the RUF with the knowledge of the Accused. NPFL radio operators were sent to Sierra Leone and trained RUF fighters in radio communication. Some of these radio operators stayed in Sierra Leone following the break with the NPFL in Operation Top Final, and the RUF continued to benefit from the training and equipment provided

by the NPFL throughout the conflict in Sierra Leone and during the Indictment period.

78. The Accused gave Sam Bockarie a satellite phone in October 1998. Bockarie also received "top up cards" for phone credit from Benjamin Yeaten. The Accused also gave a satellite phone to Issa Sesay in 2000, albeit with full knowledge of the ECOWAS leaders. The supply of such satellite phones enhanced the communications capability of both Bockarie and Sesay, which they used in furtherance of RUF and RUF/AFRC military activities. Sesay, for example, used a satellite phone to report to Bockarie that Kono was under RUF control. While Foday Sankoh was also given a satellite phone, the Prosecution failed to prove that the phone came from the Accused.

79. In addition to providing communications training and equipment to the RUF, the Accused and his subordinates facilitated communications for the RUF through their own communications network. The RUF/AFRC was provided access to radio communications equipment in Liberia by the Accused or his subordinates. This equipment was used by RUF radio operators to communicate with the RUF, in one instance concerning supplies of military equipment, and in another to update Bockarie on events in Sierra Leone when he was in Liberia. A radio was provided by the Accused to Johnny Paul Koroma. However, this radio was used specifically for the purpose of enabling Koroma to communicate with the West Side Boys about the UN peacekeepers that they had taken hostage. The evidence did not establish that the Accused and Yeaten received updates during the Freetown invasion from an RUF operator stationed in Liberia.

80. Although the establishment of the infrastructure and the training of RUF radio operators occurred prior to the Indictment period, the ongoing support from the Accused and his subordinates through the provision of satellite phones, the use of the NPFL communications

infrastructure, and the transmission of "448" messages alerting the RUF to imminent ECOMOG attack, collectively enhanced the communications capacity of the RUF/AFRC during the Indictment period, and its capacity to carry out military operations in which crimes were committed.

81. In relation to the guesthouse, the Trial Chamber finds that from 1998 to 2001 the Accused provided a base for the RUF in Monrovia, equipped with a long-range radio and telephone, RUF radio operators, SSS security supervised by Benjamin Yeaten, cooks and a caretaker. Although the guesthouse was used by RUF members partly for matters relevant to the peace process or for diplomatic purposes, it was also used to facilitate the transfer of arms, ammunition and funds directly from the Accused to the RUF, and the delivery of diamonds from the RUF directly to the Accused, belying his testimony that he 19was entirely unaware of what occurred at the guesthouse. The RUF guesthouse provided a base for the RUF in Monrovia, which facilitated the regular transfers of arms and ammunition from the Accused to the RUF, as well as diamonds from the RUF to the Accused, transactions which played a vital role in the military operations of the RUF in which crimes were committed.

82. The Trial Chamber further finds that during the Indictment period, the Accused provided much needed road and air transportation to the RUF of arms and ammunition into RUF territory. Materiel was also escorted across military checkpoints by security personnel working for the Accused, including Daniel Tamba (a.k.a. Jungle), Joseph Marzah (a.k.a. Zigzag), and Sampson Weah. This facilitation of road and air transportation of materiel, as well as security escorts, played a vital role in the operations of the RUF/AFRC during a period when an international arms embargo was in force.

83. The Accused also provided financial support, military training, technical support and other operational support to the RUF, including medical support. In most instances in which the Accused provided financial support, the funds given by the Accused to various individuals were for unspecified or personal use. The evidence failed to establish that the 10 million CFA francs given by the Accused to the RUF in Côte d'Ivoire, or the $USD 15,000 given by him to Sesay to support the RUF, were used to facilitate arms and diamond deals. However, the Accused did give funds to Bockarie, in the tens of thousands of dollars, to buy arms and ammunition from ULIMO. The RUF received financial support for arms and ammunition from sources other than the Accused as well.

84. Similarly, while the Accused provided other forms of support to the RUF, including medical support, and he acknowledged that he permitted injured RUF fighters to get treatment in Liberia, it is not clear how continuous or substantial the provision of medical care was throughout the Indictment period. In preparation for the Fitti-Fatta mission in mid-1998, the Accused sent 'herbalists' who marked fighters in Buedu and in Kono in order to bolster their confidence for the mission to recapture Kono. Other support included the provision of goods such as food, clothing, cigarettes, alcohol and other supplies to the RUF by the Accused. The evidence is insufficient to enable the Trial 20

Chamber to judge the quantity of supplies provided. Other supplies for the RUF came from Liberia through other channels unrelated to the Accused.

85. With regard to military training and technical support, the Accused instructed Bockarie in 1998 to open a training base in Bunumbu, Kailahun District, and told him also in 1998 that the RUF should construct or re-prepare an airfield in Buedu. However, the Prosecution

failed to prove that the Accused sent Martina Johnson, a former NPFL artillery commander, to Buedu to train RUF fighters to use a 40-barrel missile gun.

86. The Accused provided safe haven to RUF fighters, including Mike Lamin, when they crossed into Liberia after the retreat from Zogoda in 1996, but the Accused was not found to have ordered the RUF combatants to cross into Liberia. He had not yet taken office as President at that time, however, and the Prosecution failed to prove that he facilitated documentation to enable Lamin to travel to Côte d'Ivoire.

Arms and Ammunition

87. Turning to the allegations of the Prosecution relating to the role of the Accused in providing military support to the RUF/AFRC, the Trial Chamber first considered two preliminary issues raised by the Defence, one relating to the status of the border between Sierra Leone and Liberia, and the other relating to disarmament in Liberia.

The Trial Chamber finds that at no relevant time in the Indictment period was the ECOMOG presence on the Liberia/Sierra Leone border, or the official closure of the border by the Liberian government, sufficient to prevent the cross-border movement of arms and ammunition.

With regard to the claim that as a result of disarmament and the destruction of arms, as well as the arms embargo, Liberia had insufficient arms and ammunition to supply Sierra Leone, the Trial Chamber finds that despite these measures, the Accused was able to obtain arms and had the capacity to supply arms and ammunitions from Liberia to the rebel groups in Sierra Leone.

Moreover, he had the capacity to facilitate larger arms shipments through third countries. Of the arms shipments to the RUF and AFRC linked to the Accused during the Indictment period, the largest arrived not from Liberia, but through Liberia from third party states, primarily Burkina Faso. 21

88. The Accused directly supplied arms and ammunition to the RUF/ AFRC, as well as facilitating the supply of arms and ammunition to the RUF/AFRC from outside Liberia. During the Junta period, the Accused sent ammunition to Bockarie via Daniel Tamba (a.k.a. Jungle) in 1997.

The Accused was the source of the materiel delivered by Tamba, Joseph (a.k.a Zizgag) Marzah and Sampson Weah, among others, to Sierra Leone throughout 1998 and 1999, such supplies consisting of both arms and ammunition. Bockarie himself made trips to Liberia in 1998 and 1999 during which he obtained arms and ammunition from the Accused.

During Issa Sesay's leadership of the RUF, the Accused continued to deliver arms and ammunition to the RUF in 2000 and 2001 via Tamba, Marzah, Weah and others. Sesay himself made trips to Liberia, including a trip in May 2000 and at least two trips in the second half of 2000 and early 2001, during which he obtained arms and ammunition from the Accused.

89. Although the materiel delivered through, inter alia, Tamba, Weah and Marzah was limited in quantity, certain shipments provided by the Accused on Bockarie's trips to Liberia in 1998 and 1999 did contain sizeable amounts of materiel.

90. After 14 February 1998, the Accused sent Varmuyan Sherif to open a corridor between Lofa County and RUF-held territories to facilitate the trade of arms and ammunition between the RUF/AFRC

and ULIMO. As a result, members of ULIMO who were supposed to disarm and surrender their arms to the UN, instead sold or bartered hem to the RUF. The Accused also provided financial support to the RUF/AFRC in order to facilitate their purchases of arms and ammunition from ex-ULIMO combatants.

However, the evidence was insufficient to establish that the Accused attempted to help the RUF purchase arms and ammunition from ECOMOG and ULIMO prior to the Junta period.

91. The Accused facilitated two large shipments of ammunition. The first occurred in late 1997. In around September 1997, the Accused sent Ibrahim Bah to Freetown to meet with Sam Bockarie and Johnny Paul Koroma to make arrangements for the procurement of arms and ammunition. Bah was given 90 carats of diamonds and $USD 90,000 to pay for the shipment. This shipment of arms and ammunition was delivered by plane to 22 Magburaka in Sierra Leone sometime between September and December 1997 and was distributed amongst members of the AFRC/RUF Junta. Materiel from this shipment was used by the AFRC/RUF forces in fighting ECOMOG and SLPP forces in Freetown before, during and after the Intervention, in the Junta mining operations at Tongo Fields prior to the ECOMOG Intervention, in "Operation Pay Yourself" and subsequent offensives on Kono, as well as in the commission of crimes during those operations.

92. The Accused also facilitated a shipment of materiel around November 1998 from Burkina Faso. Ibrahim Bah and Musa Cissé, Charles Taylor's Chief of Protocol, accompanied a delegation led by Bockarie to Burkina Faso where a shipment of arms and ammunition was arranged and brought back by plane to Liberia, and then transported by trucks provided by the Accused to Sierra Leone.

The Trial Chamber finds that the Accused was instrumental in procuring and transporting this large quantity of arms and ammunition for the RUF, that he was paid for it with diamonds, and that he kept some of the shipment for his own purposes. The shipment from Burkina Faso was unprecedented in volume and, as noted previously, was critical in the December 1998 and January 1999 offensives.

93. The Trial Chamber considered the Defence submission that other sources of military equipment for the RUF and AFRC far outweighed supplies allegedly provided by the Accused. In addition to receiving arms and ammunition from the Accused, the RUF and the AFRC also obtained supplies from the existing stockpiles of the former government when they took over power in May 1997, by capturing them from ECOMOG and UN peacekeepers, and through trade with ULIMO, AFL and ECOMOG commanders.

However, these sources of materiel were of minor importance in comparison to those supplied or facilitated by the Accused. Significantly, the RUF/AFRC in fact heavily and frequently relied on the materiel supplied and facilitated by the Accused; the Accused's support often satisfied a need or request for materiel at a particular time; and shipments of materiel supplied by or facilitated by the Accused often contributed to and were causally linked to the capture of further supplies by the RUF and AFRC.

Although there were instances in which the materiel that the Accused gave to the RUF/AFRC was more limited in quantity, on a number of occasions the arms and 23ammunition which he supplied or facilitated were indispensable for the RUF/AFRC military offensives. The materiel provided or facilitated by the Accused was critical in enabling the operational strategy of the RUF and the AFRC during the Indictment period.

94. On the basis of its findings, more detailed in the written Judgement, the Trial Chamber rejects the Defence argument that Benjamin Yeaten, the Director of the Accused's Special Security Service, to whom the arms couriers reported, was engaged in the trade of arms and ammunition for the RUF independently and without the knowledge of the Accused.

Military Personnel

95. As previously noted, approximately 20 former NPFL fighters who had been integrated into the Armed Forces of Liberia formed part of a group of approximately 200 fighters led by O-Five who attacked and committed crimes in Karina and Kamalo in Bombali District on or about August/September 1998.

Subsequently, this group of 20 fighters was incorporated into the Red Lion Battalion, which was comprised of 200 fighters and was part of a larger group of up to approximately 1,000 fighters who attacked and committed crimes in Waterloo, Fisher Lane, Hastings, Freetown Eastern Police, Pademba Road Prison, Kingtom, Fourah Bay and Upgun in Freetown and the Western Area, on or about December1998/ January 1999.

These 20 fighters were sent by the Accused from Liberia to Sierra Leone where they joined the RUF/AFRC forces in Sierra Leone and participated in attacks in which crimes were committed.

96. The Trial Chamber finds that Abu Keita and the reinforcements known as the Scorpion Unit were sent by the Accused to Sierra Leone and participated in the attack on Kenema, in which Abu Keita committed crimes. The Kenema attack was part of the attack on Kono and Freetown.

Although the evidence did not establish beyond reasonable doubt that the Scorpion Unit was sent for the purpose of fighting in the Kono and Freetown military operations, which included Kenema, Daniel Tamba, on behalf of the Accused, approved Bockarie's decision to integrate the Scorpion Unit under his command.24

97. The Accused sent former SLA soldiers to the Bunumbu training camp soon after the Intervention, although their subsequent deployment was not established. The Accused later sent a group of former SLA soldiers from Liberia back to Sierra Leone to support the attack on Freetown.

These men arrived in Kailahun in or around late November 1998, and they participated in the attack on Kono in December 1998, although they were unable to reach Freetown and did not participate in the Freetown attack.

98. Liberian government authorities and RUF/AFRC members recruited and forced Sierra Leonean refugees residing in Liberia to return to Sierra Leone to fight. However, the evidence did not establish that these civilian refugees participated in attacks in Sierra Leone.

99. The Trial Chamber considered the allegation by the Prosecution that the Accused assisted the AFRC/RUF by capturing and returning AFRC/RUF deserters to Sierra Leone. The Trial Chamber finds that the Liberian police authorities detained two RUF/AFRC members Fonti Kanu, and Dauda Aruna Fornie, and handed them over to RUF personnel in late 1998 and late 1999, respectively. In evidence about his own arrest and torture in Sierra Leone, Mohammed Kabbah described as common knowledge the cooperation of Liberian authorities and the RUF on the return of wanted Sierra Leoneans who escaped to Liberia.

Diamonds

100. The Trial Chamber finds that there was a continuous supply by the AFRC/RUF of diamonds mined from areas in Sierra Leone to the Accused, often in exchange for arms and ammunition.

101. During the period May 1997 to February 1998 diamonds mined in Kono and Tongo Fields were delivered from the AFRC/RUF to the Accused by Daniel Tamba (a.k.a. Jungle) in exchange for arms and ammunition.

102. Following the ECOMOG Intervention, from February 1998 to July 1999, the diamonds delivered to the Accused by Sam Bockarie directly, as well as indirectly through intermediaries such as Eddie Kanneh and Daniel Tamba, were given to him in 25order to get arms and ammunition from him, or sometimes for "safekeeping" on behalf of the RUF.

103. From February 1998 to July 1999, diamonds were delivered to the Accused by Sam Bockarie directly. These diamonds were delivered to the Accused for the purpose of obtaining arms and ammunitions from him. During this period, diamonds were also delivered through intermediaries such as Eddie Kanneh and Daniel Tamba.

104. The RUF also traded diamonds with entities and individuals other than the Accused or his government. Testimonial evidence of specific involvement of the Accused in the trade of diamonds supported the findings of a United Nations report of a panel of experts that diamond smuggling from Sierra Leone to Liberia was "the bulk of the RUF trade in diamonds" and while difficult to quantify was nevertheless the "primary source of income to the RUF". This report concluded that the trade of diamonds between Liberia and Sierra Leone could not be

conducted in Liberia "without the permission and the involvement of government officials at the highest level."

105. From July 1999 to May 2000, Foday Sankoh delivered diamonds to the Accused, and diamonds were delivered to the Accused on his behalf in or before 1999 while he was in detention. In March 2000, Foday Sankoh visited South Africa and travelled through Monrovia on his way back to Sierra Leone, meeting with the Accused in Monrovia. According to one witness, among the diamonds delivered to the Accused during this meeting were a 45 carat diamond and two 25 carat diamonds.

106. From June 2000 until the end of hostilities in 2002, Issa Sesay delivered diamonds to the Accused, including on one occasion a 36 carat diamond. Eddie Kanneh also delivered diamonds to the Accused on Sesay's behalf. Sometimes the diamonds were delivered to the Accused supposedly for "safekeeping" until Sankoh's release from detention and, at other times, in exchange for supplies and/or arms and ammunition.

During this period, diamond trading between the RUF and persons other than the Accused also took place. 26

107. As detailed in documentary evidence before the Trial Chamber, Liberian

Diamonds are generally known to be of a significantly lower quality than diamonds from Sierra Leone, refuting the claim made by the Accused that he would have had no reason to trade in diamonds from Sierra Leone because Liberia had its own diamonds. Moreover, the documentary evidence indicates that export of diamonds from Liberia was far greater than Liberian diamond production, attributing the difference to diamonds from Sierra Leone smuggled through Liberia.

108. The Trial Chamber finds that the Accused also facilitated a relationship between the RUF and a Belgian known as Alpha Bravo for the purpose of diamond transactions. However, there was insufficient evidence to establish that the Accused facilitated a relationship between the RUF and other diamond dealers.

109. The Accused also provided diesel fuel for the Caterpillars at the diamond mining sites in Sierra Leone, and equipment for use in mining diamonds to the RUF on at least one occasion between 1998 and 2002. While there may have been multiple sources of mining equipment and fuel entering Sierra Leone during the Indictment period, the Accused was among them. The Trial Chamber has also found that men sent by the Accused visited at least one mining site and assessed mining operations.

110. While there was evidence of occasional inquiries from Benjamin Yeaten and reports to him about the activity at the mining sites in Sierra Leone, the evidence did not establish that regular updates were sent to the Accused about mining activity.

The Peace Process

111. The Trial Chamber will now summarize its findings relating to the role of the Accused in the peace process and the Defence contention that his involvement with the RUF/AFRC was solely for the purpose of promoting peace.

112. During a radio conversation with Foday Sankoh, following the attack on Sierra Rutile in 1994, the Accused advised the RUF leader to send an External Delegation to Côte d'Ivoire. In Côte d'Ivoire, the delegates met Musa Cissé, an NPFL representative, who allowed them to use his radio for communications with Sankoh. The Accused, 27through contact with Musa Cissé, invited members of the

External Delegation to Liberia, where he met them twice in 1995. In December 1995 the Accused met members of the External Delegation in Cote d'Ivoire on the occasion of the publication of "Footpaths to Democracy", at which time he gave them CFA 10 million francs for their maintenance.

113. The Accused instructed Foday Sankoh to participate in the Abidjan peace talks from March to November 1996 in order to obtain ammunition and materiel for the RUF. The evidence established that while in Abidjan, Sankoh obtained arms and ammunition for the RUF using funds from Libya. However, the evidence was insufficient to establish that Sankoh used contacts of the Accused to obtain arms and ammunition in Abidjan.

114. The Accused played an active role in the Lomé peace negotiations, which role the Prosecution alleged to be subversive, suggesting that the Accused improperly assisted and advised the RUF delegation before and during the negotiations so as to procure the most favourable outcome for RUF/AFRC and himself. The Trial Chamber did not find this to be the case, in the absence of evidence that the Accused controlled the RUF delegation or dictated the outcome of the negotiations.

However, the evidence established that the Accused was engaged in arms transactions at the same time that he was involved in the peace negotiations in Lomé, publicly promoting peace at the Lomé negotiations while privately providing arms and ammunition to the RUF.

115. Following the Lomé Peace Accord, the so-called West Side Boys, discontent with the apparent exclusion of the AFRC from the peace process, kidnapped UN peacekeepers and others in Sierra Leone and demanded to talk to, and then see, Johnny Paul Koroma, their leader.

The Accused officially and publicly made arrangements to bring Koroma to Monrovia, including negotiating a waiver of the UN travel ban, and facilitating several meetings, thereby playing a central role in bringing Koroma and Sankoh together and achieving a reduction in the tension between the RUF and the AFRC. The evidence establishes, as the Accused contends, that the UN and ECOWAS Heads of State knew about his public role in the negotiations. Taylor's influence with both Koroma and Sankoh evidently made him a significant actor in the process and helped to facilitate the 28 release of the UN peacekeepers and others who had been taken captive by the West Side Boys.

116. The Trial Chamber accepts that as President of Liberia, as a member of the ECOWAS Committee of Five (later Committee of Six), the Accused wielded considerable influence over the warring factions in Sierra Leone and that the ECOWAS heads of state played a substantial role in the Sierra Leone peace process. However, there is strong evidence showing that while publicly participating in regional efforts to broker peace in Sierra Leone, the Accused was secretly fuelling hostilities between the AFRC/RUF and the democratically elected authorities in Sierra Leone.

This clandestine undermining of the peace process by the Accused occurred even when he knew that an arms embargo by the UN and ECOWAS was in force in the region.

117. In late April or early May 2000, the RUF forcibly disarmed and detained a group of approximately 500 UNAMSIL peacekeepers in Sierra Leone. The Accused was asked by ECOWAS to become involved in negotiations for the release of these hostages, and his mandate was endorsed by the United Nations. Thereafter, the Accused invited Issa Sesay, RUF interim leader, to Monrovia to discuss the matter of their release. After this meeting, from about the middle to the end of May

2000, the RUF released the captured UNAMSIL peacekeepers into Liberian territory in stages.

The Trial Chamber found that the Accused had significant influence over the RUF decision to release the UN peacekeepers, and that in his meeting with Issa Sesay, Taylor promised him assistance "in the struggle". While the Trial Chamber found that Issa Sesay made a trip to Liberia in May 2000 in which he obtained arms and ammunition from the Accused, the evidence was insufficient to establish that this materiel was provided in exchange for Issa Sesay agreeing to release the UNAMSIL peacekeepers.

118. In July 2000, a meeting was convened in Monrovia to discuss the selection of new leadership for the RUF following Sankoh's imprisonment. The meeting was attended by all of the ECOWAS heads of state and an RUF delegation led by Issa Sesay where it was proposed that Sesay take over as Interim Leader of the RUF. In another meeting late that night, the Accused privately advised Issa Sesay to say that he would disarm but "not do it 29in reality". At that time, the Accused was supplying Sesay with arms and ammunition, and also calling on the RUF to send forces to help him fight his own enemies together with the AFL in Liberia and in Guinea.

119. The Trial Chamber accordingly finds that while the Accused publicly played a substantial role in the Sierra Leone peace process, including as a member of the ECOWAS Committee of Five (later Committee of Six), secretly he was fuelling hostilities between the AFRC/RUF and the democratically elected authorities in Sierra Leone, by urging the former not to disarm and actively providing them with arms and ammunition, acting, as the Prosecution described, as "a two-headed Janus".

Leadership and Command Structure

120. The Trial Chamber has considered the leadership and command structure of the RUF, and the role of the Accused, if any, in relation to that structure.

The Trial Chamber has found that Foday Sankoh and the Accused met in Libya in the early 1990s and pursued parallel goals and aspirations, but not in a chain of command. Following Operation Top Final in 1992 and the withdrawal of NPFL troops from Sierra Leone, contacts and cooperation between the Accused and Sankoh continued, but to a lesser extent.

The Accused asked Sankoh to send troops in 1993 to help him fight ULIMO. He advised Sankoh prior to and following the RUF attack on Sierra Rutile, and he advised Sankoh to send an External Delegation to Cote d'Ivoire.

121. When Foday Sankoh was arrested in Nigeria in March 1997, he instructed Sam Bockarie to take orders from the Accused.

While much evidence was adduced relating to the trade of arms and diamonds between Sam Bockarie and the Accused, the evidence did not establish that Bockarie took orders from the Accused.

The instructions given to Bockarie by the Accused were given with the inherent authority the Accused had by virtue of his position. Bockarie was deferential to the Accused and generally followed his instruction.

However, the Trial Chamber considers that the role Sankoh envisioned for the Accused while he was in detention was that he would guide Bockarie, and that Bockarie should look to his guidance, not that the

Accused should take over Sankoh's role as the leader of the RUF with effective control over its actions. 30

122. Sometime around March 1998, Sam Bockarie was promoted. The Prosecution alleged that this promotion was made by the Accused directly, or through a joint decision between himself and Johnny Paul Koroma. Bockarie had just returned from Monrovia.

The Trial Chamber finds that the Accused may well have been consulted by Koroma, or talked directly with Bockarie about the promotion while he was in Monrovia, but not that Bockarie was promoted by the Accused.

Like Sankoh, Koroma turned to the Accused for advice and support, and the Trial Chamber accepts that he would have consulted the Accused. Nevertheless, the Accused was not part of the command structure.

123. In December 1999, Sam Bockarie left Sierra Leone and went to Liberia, amidst violent clashes between RUF fighters loyal to Foday Sankoh and RUF fighters loyal to him. He was told to leave Sierra Leone by the Accused, but the Trial Chamber finds that in summoning Bockarie to Liberia, the Accused relied on the authority of ECOWAS and sought the help of President Obasanjo, organizing a meeting at Roberts International Airport between Foday Sankoh, Sam Bockarie, President Obasanjo and himself, as a result of which a decision was made that Bockarie would not return to Sierra Leone until the disarmament process had been completed.

124. On 26 July 2000 a meeting took place at the Executive Mansion in Monrovia between the heads of state of ECOWAS and an RUF delegation led by Issa Sesay, where the suggestion was made that Issa Sesay should become the Interim Leader of the RUF. Sesay would not

accept the appointment without it first being approved by the RUF and Foday Sankoh. A meeting of RUF commanders was held, and a letter was also delivered to Foday Sankoh by President Obasanjo seeking Sankoh's consent to the appointment.

At a follow up meeting in August 2000, Sesay was confirmed as the RUF Interim Leader. Presidents Obasanjo and Konare both met with Sankoh in Freetown, without the Accused present, and the Trial Chamber finds that this process was undertaken by ECOWAS heads of state collectively, rather than the Accused unilaterally.

125. The Accused called on the AFRC/RUF to assist him in fighting outside Sierra Leone. In 1999, the Accused ordered Bockarie to send AFRC/RUF forces to assist him in his fight against Mosquito Spray and the LURD forces that had attacked his forces. In 312000 and 2001 the Accused instructed Issa Sesay to send RUF forces. The RUF forces sent in response to these requests fought alongside AFL forces in Liberia and Guinea under the command of the Accused's subordinates. The evidence was insufficient to establish that in 2001, Bockarie left Liberia to fight for Taylor's allies in Cote d'Ivoire, as alleged by the Prosecution. Knowledge of the Accused of Crimes Committed in Sierra Leone.

126. The Accused testified that prior to becoming President, he was not following whether crimes were committed by the RUF in Sierra Leone. The Trial Chamber found that the relationship of the Accused with the RUF from 1989 until he became President was much closer than he admitted. The Accused knew that during the early war years in Sierra Leone, RUF soldiers, under the command of NPFL officers, abducted civilians including children, forcing them to fight within the NPFL/ RUF forces against the Sierra Leonean forces and ULIMO. Moreover, the Accused was aware that the RUF captured civilians and looted

money during the attack on Sierra Rutile, and he advised Sankoh on the use of the hostages and the money.

127. The Accused testified that, upon becoming President, he received a daily briefing from his national security advisor, which would include press and intelligence reports. Also, following his election, the Accused joined the ECOWAS Committee of Five and would therefore have received and read ECOWAS reports. The numerous reports prepared in 1997 by ECOWAS and the United Nations agencies establish that, as early as May 1997, the crimes committed by the Junta were significantly reported by these international organisations. In a report of June 1997, the United Nations Department of Humanitarian Affairs reported killings of civilians, amputations and looting in Sierra Leone.

An ECOWAS report of the Committee of Four on the situation in Sierra Leone, in August 1997, described the "massive looting of property, murder and rapes" following the coup on 25 May 1997. The final report of the sixteenth meeting of ECOWAS Chiefs of State in Abuja, Nigeria, in August 1997, a meeting in which the Liberian representative participated, also described "a very bloody coup, followed by massive looting and vandalisation of public and private properties and the opening of the prisons by the junta". In a speech to the Nation on 18 June 1997, the RUF forces themselves 32 apologised for the atrocities they had committed in Sierra Leone, including killings and rapes.

128. Following the coup, on 29 August 1997 ECOWAS decided to place a total embargo on all supplies of petroleum products, arms and military equipment to Sierra Leone. Similarly, on 8 October 1997, the United Nations Security Council decided to impose an embargo on arms and ammunitions to Sierra Leone.

These embargos clearly indicate that, at the very latest by August 1997, the Junta was perceived by the international community as a threat to peace and it was recognized that military support could facilitate the commission of the crimes described above.

129. The Accused was evasive in his testimony as to what and when he knew about the crimes being committed in Sierra Leone. In light of these contemporary reports, and considering the fact that the Accused received daily briefings from his national security advisor about the international situation and was a member of the ECOWAS Committee of Five, the Trial Chamber finds that as early as August 1997, Charles Taylor was informed in detail of the crimes committed during the Junta period including murder, abduction of civilians including children, rape, amputation and looting.

130. After 1997, the media coverage of the AFRC/RUF's crimes and terror campaign against the Sierra Leonean civilian population increased. Many reports and articles by International Organisations, Non Governmental Organisations and newspapers admitted into evidence describe the atrocities committed by the AFRC/RUF troops after the ECOMOG Intervention and the end of the Junta Government. These public reports demonstrate that at that time, it was public knowledge that AFRC/RUF forces committed the following crimes: unlawful killings, sexual violence, physical violence, looting, conscription and use of child soldiers, abduction, terrorism, and other atrocities.

131. The Accused himself admitted that by April 1998 if "someone was providing support to the AFRC/RUF", he "would be supporting a group engaged in a campaign of atrocities against the civilian population of Sierra Leone". At that time, as the Accused testified, there were news reports of a "horrific campaign being waged against the civilian population in Sierra Leone." In a statement dated July 1998,

the Accused "strongly 33condemned the continuing rebel activities in Sierra Leone, as well as the horrendous atrocities that had been committed there."

132. Based on this evidence, and the testimony of the Accused himself, the Trial Chamber finds that the Accused was aware of the crimes committed by RUF/AFRC forces against civilians, including murder, abduction of civilian including children, rape, amputation and looting, as early as August 1997 when he became President of Liberia.

Summary of Legal Findings

133. The Indictment charges the Accused with individual criminal responsibility pursuant to Article 6.1 of the Statute for the crimes referred to in Articles 2, 3 and 4 of the Statute alleged in the Indictment. The Trial Chamber has found that the crimes charged under Counts 1 to 11 of the Indictment were committed and now turns to the responsibility of the Accused for these crimes.

Responsibility Pursuant to Article 6(3) of the Statute

134. The Indictment charges that the Accused is individually criminally responsible for the crimes referred to in Articles 2, 3 and 4 of the Statute as alleged in the Indictment by virtue of holding positions of superior responsibility and exercising command and control over subordinate members of the RUF, AFRC, AFRC/RUF Junta or alliance, and/or Liberian fighters. It is alleged that the Accused is responsible for the criminal acts of his subordinates in that he knew or had reason to know that the subordinate was about to commit such acts or had done so and the Accused failed to take the necessary and reasonable measures to prevent such acts or to punish the perpetrators thereof.

135. The Accused denies criminal responsibility based on a superior/subordinate relationship with the perpetrators of the crimes.

136. Article 6(3) holds a superior criminally responsible if the superior knew or had reason to know that his or her subordinate was about to commit crimes prohibited by the Statute or had done so, and the superior failed to take the necessary and reasonable measures to prevent or punish the perpetrators. It must thus be demonstrated that the 34superior had effective "command and control" over his subordinates—i.e. the material ability to prevent or punish the commission of the offence.

137. The Trial Chamber is of the view that the Accused had substantial influence over the leadership of the RUF, and to a lesser extent that of the AFRC. However, that substantial influence over the conduct of others fell short of "effective command and control" as demonstrated by the evidence.

138. The evidence establishes that from 1990 to March 1997 Sankoh was the sole leader of the RUF and that he did not take orders from the Accused. When Sankoh was arrested in March 1997 he appointed Bockarie to lead the RUF and instructed him to take direction from the Accused.

139. The Trial Chamber finds that the Accused gave guidance, advice and direction to Bockarie and to his successor, Issa Sesay, but that the evidence does not establish that either of them was a subordinate of the Accused, nor that the Accused had effective command and control over the RUF during their respective tenures. Similarly, the Trial Chamber finds that the Accused gave guidance, advice and direction to Johnny Paul Koroma when he was leader of the AFRC/RUF Junta, but the evidence does not establish that he was a subordinate of the Accused,

nor that the Accused had effective command and control over the AFRC/RUF Junta.

140. With regard to Liberian fighters who were found to have participated in the commission of crimes, the Trial Chamber finds that even if they were sent to Sierra Leone by the Accused, there is insufficient evidence to find beyond a reasonable doubt that they remained under the effective command and control of the Accused once in Sierra Leone.

141. The Trial Chamber accordingly finds that the Prosecution failed to prove beyond reasonable doubt that the Accused is individually criminally responsible under Article 6(3) for the crimes referred to in Articles 2, 3 and 4 of the Statute as alleged in the Indictment.35

Joint Criminal Enterprise

142. The Indictment charges the Accused with the crimes referred to in Articles 2, 3 and 4 of the Statute as alleged in the Indictment, which crimes amounted to or were involved within a common plan, design or purpose in which the Accused participated, or were a reasonably foreseeable consequence of such common plan, design or purpose.

143. As discussed earlier, the Trial Chamber found that the Prosecution failed to prove that any of the three alleged meetings in Libya, Burkina Faso and Voinjama, where the common plan is said to have been established, took place. Furthermore, while the Trial

Chamber found that the Accused provided significant operational and military support to the RUF, particularly after he became President of Liberia, the evidence does not establish that this support was provided pursuant to a common plan in the context of a joint criminal enterprise.

144. Accordingly, the Trial Chamber finds that the Prosecution has failed to prove beyond a reasonable doubt that the Accused is criminally responsible by virtue of having participated in a common plan, design or purpose to commit the crimes alleged in the Indictment.

Responsibility under Article 6(1) for Aiding and Abetting

145. The Indictment charges that the Accused, by his acts or omissions, is individually criminally responsible pursuant to Article 6.1 of the Statute for (inter alia) aiding and abetting the planning, preparation or execution of the crimes referred to in Articles 2, 3 and 4 of the Statute as alleged in the Indictment.

146. The Prosecution submits that in providing practical assistance, encouragement, or moral support, the Accused's acts had a substantial effect on the perpetration of the crimes charged in the Indictment, and that he had a clear intent to act in support of those crimes.

147. The Defence denies that the Accused is responsible for aiding and abetting the commission of any of the crimes charged in the Indictment. 36

148. "Aiding and abetting" requires that the accused gave practical assistance, encouragement, or moral support which had a substantial effect on the perpetration of a crime.

149. The Trial Chamber finds beyond reasonable doubt that the Accused provided arms and ammunition, military personnel, operational support, moral support and ongoing guidance to the RUF, AFRC, AFRC/RUF Junta or alliance, and Liberian fighters for military operations during the Indictment period. Commission of crimes intrinsic to the RUF/AFRC's war strategy.

150. Before turning to the various forms of assistance provided by the Accused, the Trial Chamber considered the RUF/AFRC's war strategy. Throughout the Indictment period, the operational strategy of the RUF and AFRC was characterised by a campaign of crimes against the Sierra Leonean civilian population, including murders, rapes, sexual slavery, looting, abductions, forced labor, conscription of child soldiers, amputations and other forms of physical violence and acts of terror.

These crimes were inextricably linked to how the RUF and AFRC achieved their political and military objectives. In particular, under the leadership of Sam Bockarie, the RUF and AFRC pursued a policy of committing crimes in order to achieve military gains at any civilian cost, and also politically in order to attract the attention of the international community and to heighten their negotiating stance with the Sierra Leonean government.

That their operations were given titles such as "Operation No Living Thing", and "Operation Spare No Soul" made explicit the intent of the RUF and AFRC to wage a campaign of terror against civilians as part of their war strategy.

151. The findings of the Trial Chamber as to the various forms of assistance provided by the Accused are as follows.

Arms and Ammunition

152. During the Indictment period, the Accused directly or through intermediaries supplied or facilitated the supply of arms and ammunition to the RUF/AFRC. The Accused sent small but regular supplies of arms and ammunition and other supplies to the 37 RUF from late 1997 to 1998 via his subordinates, and substantial amounts of arms and ammunition to the AFRC/RUF from 1998 to 2001. The Accused facilitated much larger shipments of arms and ammunition

from third party states to the AFRC/RUF, including the Magburaka shipment of October 1997 and the Burkina Faso shipment of

November/December 1998.

153. Also during the Indictment period, these arms and ammunition were used by the RUF, AFRC, AFRC/RUF Junta or alliance, and Liberian fighters in military operations, including the Junta mining operations at Tongo Fields prior to the ECOMOG Intervention, "Operation Pay Yourself" and subsequent offensives in Kono District in 1998, and in the Freetown invasion in January 1999, and attacks on the outskirts of Freetown and the Western Area in late January to early February 1999. These operations involved widespread or systematic attacks on the civilian population and the commission of crimes. The Trial Chamber finds that the provision and facilitation of these arms and ammunition constituted practical assistance which had a substantial effect on the perpetration of crimes by the RUF and RUF/AFRC during the Indictment period.

Military Personnel

154. The Accused also provided military personnel to the RUF/AFRC. The Accused provided a group of 20 ex-NPFL fighters who had been integrated into the AFL. These 20 fighters fought in Karina and Kamalo in Bombali District in August/September 1998 as part of a group of 200 fighters. These 20 fighters were later on incorporated into the Red Lion Battalion, which comprised of 200 fighters. The Red Lion Battalion was part of a group of 1,000 fighters who participated in the invasion of Freetown and committed crimes during the course of military operations in December 1998/January 1999. 155. The Accused reorganized, armed and sent former SLA fighters and Sierra Leonean civilians who had retreated to Liberia back to Sierra Leone to fight in

the Kono and Freetown operation, and these men fought in the Kono operation in December 1998. 38

156. Moreover, the Accused sent Abu Keita and 150 fighters as reinforcements known as the Scorpion Unit, who participated in the attack on Kono and Kenema Districts in late 1998/early 1999.

157. The Trial Chamber finds that the practical assistance provided by these military personnel sent by the Accused had a substantial effect on the commission of crimes by the RUF/AFRC during the course of military operations. Operational Support

158. In the pre-Indictment period, NPFL radio operators and equipment were sent to Sierra Leone, and RUF fighters were trained by the NPFL radio operators in radio communications, with the knowledge of the Accused. The RUF continued to benefit into the Indictment period from the enhanced communications capacity that resulted from this assistance. However, as the acts of the Accused took place prior to the Indictment period, the Trial Chamber has not taken them into account in determining criminal responsibility.

159. The Trial Chamber found that the Accused also provided operational support to the RUF/AFRC during the Indictment period, including giving Sam Bockarie and Issa Sesay satellite phones, and facilitating communications for the RUF through the NPFL's own communications network; providing the RUF/AFRC access to radio communications equipment in Liberia; allowing the use of the radio station at Benjamin Yeaten's home for communications with Bockarie and later Sesay; and the transmission of "448 messages" to RUF forces warning them of impending ECOMOG jet attacks, which the Accused must have known about. This communications support provided practical assistance to the RUF/AFRC for the crimes committed during

the course of their military operations throughout the Indictment period.

160. The Accused also provided financial support to the RUF/AFRC, including funds to Bockarie of $10,000 to $20,000 at a time, on multiple occasions for the purchase of arms from ULIMO. The Accused also kept diamonds and money in "safekeeping" for the RUF/AFRC. 39

161. The Accused also provided a guesthouse to the RUF in Monrovia, which was used by the RUF to facilitate the transfer of arms and funds from the Accused to the RUF and the delivery of diamonds from the RUF to the Accused. The Trial Chamber considers that the provision of the RUF guesthouse by the Accused, as a base of operation for procurement and a way station for the transport of arms and ammunition, provided practical assistance to the RUF/AFRC for the commission of crimes committed during the course of military operations.

162. The Accused provided other forms of support to the RUF/AFRC, including the provision of security escorts, facilitation of access through checkpoints, assistance with transport of arms and ammunition by road and by air, safe haven and medical support for treatment of wounded RUF fighters in Liberia, as well as provision of goods such as food, clothing, cigarettes, alcohol and other supplies to the RUF. The Accused also sent "herbalists" who marked fighters in Buedu and Kono to "protect" them against bullets and bolster their confidence. Liberian forces also assisted the RUF/AFRC with the capture and return of deserters to Sierra Leone.

163. The provision of such support, in addition to the military support provided, constituted practical assistance to the RUF/AFRC which had

a substantial effect on the commission of crimes committed during the course of military operations.

Encouragement and Moral Support

164. The Trial Chamber has considered the ongoing communication and consultation between the Accused and the RUF/AFRC leadership, and the ongoing advice and encouragement that the Accused provided to the RUF/AFRC. He advised Sankoh to participate in the Abidjan peace talks in 1996 in order to obtain arms and ammunition for the RUF.

He instructed the RUF to open a training base in Bunumbu in 1998, and to construct an airfield in Buedu. He instructed the AFRC/RUF to capture Kono, and subsequently advised them to hold and re-capture it, as a source of revenue through diamonds that could be used to secure arms and ammunition.

The Trial Chamber has taken into account the position of authority of the Accused as an elder statesman and as President of Liberia, the deference that was accorded to him by the RUF/AFRC 40leadership and their reliance on his guidance, and the fact that his advice was generally heeded by them.

165. Taken cumulatively, and having regard to the military support provided by the Accused to the RUF/AFRC, the Trial Chamber finds that the practical assistance, encouragement and moral support provided by the Accused had a substantial effect on the commission of crimes by the RUF/AFRC during the course of military operations in Sierra Leone.

The Accused

166. The essential mental element required for aiding and abetting is that the accused knew that his acts would assist the commission of the crime by the perpetrator or that he was aware of the substantial likelihood that his acts would assist the commission of a crime by the perpetrator. In cases of specific intent crimes, such as acts of terrorism, the accused must also be aware of the specific intent of the perpetrator.

167. As discussed earlier, the Trial Chamber is satisfied that as of August 1997, the Accused knew of the atrocities being committed against civilians in Sierra Leone by the RUF/AFRC forces and of their propensity to commit crimes. Notwithstanding such knowledge, the Accused continued to provide support to the RUF and RUF/AFRC forces during the period that crimes were being committed in Sierra Leone. The Trial Chamber therefore finds beyond reasonable doubt that the Accused knew that his support to the RUF/AFRC would provide practical assistance, encouragement or moral support to them in the commission of crimes during the course of their military operations in Sierra Leone.

Conclusion

168. For the foregoing reasons, the Trial Chamber finds beyond reasonable doubt that the Accused is criminally responsible pursuant to Article 6(1) of the Statute for aiding and abetting the commission of the crimes set forth in Counts 1 to 11 of the Indictment. 41

Planning

The Accused is charged with individual criminal responsibility pursuant to Article 6.1 of the Statute for (inter alia) planning the crimes referred to in Articles 2, 3 and 4 of the Statute as alleged in the Indictment.

169. The Prosecution submits that the Accused, acting jointly with RUF, AFRC and Liberian subordinates, designed or organised the commission of crimes, at both the preparatory and execution phases, by designing a strategy for the AFRC Junta, the RUF and AFRC forces, including selecting strategic areas to attack and control, such as Kono and the capital Freetown, and organizing the delivery of arms and ammunition needed to carry out the attacks.

170. The Defence submits that the evidence put forward by the Prosecution does not show that the Accused planned the commission of crimes or was aware of the substantial likelihood of crimes as charged in the Indictment as part of the January 6 invasion of Freetown, asserting that it was the AFRC, not the RUF, who executed and planned the attack.

171. Criminal responsibility for planning requires that the accused, alone or with others, intentionally planned the criminal conduct constituting the crimes charged, with the intent that a crime be committed in the execution of that plan, or with the awareness of the substantial likelihood that a crime would be committed in the execution of that plan.

172. The Trial Chamber found that in November 1998, Sam Bockarie and the Accused designed a two-pronged attack on Kono and Kenema, with Freetown as the ultimate destination. This plan was conveyed to RUF and AFRC commanders in December 1998 at Waterworks in Kailahun District.

173. The plan designed by Bockarie and the Accused led to the attacks on Kono and Makeni. In the course of the implementation of this plan,

a small contingent of troops led by Idrissa Kamara (a.k.a. Rambo Red Goat) reached Freetown and Bockarie's forces got to the outskirts of Freetown, where they met up with the forces led by Gullit. During the 42course of the implementation of this plan, these forces committed the crimes charged in the Indictment. These crimes resulted directly from the plan made by Bockarie and the Accused in Monrovia. There was evidence that while in Monrovia, the Accused instructed Bockarie to make the operation "fearful" in order to pressure the Government of Sierra Leone into negotiations. Moreover, following the Waterworks meeting, the Accused told Bockarie during a satellite phone conversation to use "all means" to get to Freetown.

174. The Trial Chamber found that following the Waterworks meeting Bockarie told SAJ Musa to attack Freetown but SAJ Musa refused to take orders from Bockarie and continued on his own advance pursuant to a separate plan. The Trial Chamber found that Gullit took over the leadership of the troops at Benguema following the death of SAJ Musa. Bockarie then assumed effective control over Gullit and SAJ Musa's plan was abandoned for the Bockarie/Taylor plan, as conveyed by Bockarie at Waterworks. Further execution of the plan was carried out with close coordination between Bockarie and Gullit, with Gullit in frequent communication with Bockarie and with Gullit taking orders from Bockarie. In these circumstances, the Trial Chamber finds that the Bockarie/Taylor plan substantially contributed to the commission of crimes committed by Gullit's forces while Gullit was operating under Bockarie's command.

175. The Accused, having drawn up the plan with Bockarie, and having followed its implementation closely via daily communication with Bockarie, either directly or through Yeaten, was aware of its continuing evolution.

176. As mentioned previously, the Accused was well aware of the crimes committed by the AFRC/RUF forces in the course of their military operations, and that their war strategy was explicitly based on a widespread or systematic campaign of crimes against civilians. Moreover, by his instruction to make the operation "fearful", which was repeated many times by Bockarie during the course of the Freetown invasion, and by his instruction to use "all means", the Accused demonstrated his awareness of the substantial likelihood that crimes would be committed in the execution of the plan.

177. For the foregoing reasons the Trial Chamber finds beyond reasonable doubt that the Accused is criminally responsible pursuant to Article 6(1) for planning the crimes 43committed by members of the RUF, AFRC, AFRC/RUF Junta or alliance and Liberian fighters in the attacks on Kono and Makeni, in the invasion of Freetown and during the retreat from Freetown.

Ordering

178. The Trial Chamber has found that while the Accused held a position of authority amongst the RUF and RUF/AFRC, the instructions and guidance which he gave to the RUF and RUF/AFRC were generally of an advisory nature and at times were in fact not followed by the RUF/AFRC leadership. For these reasons, the Trial Chamber finds that the Accused cannot be held responsible for ordering the commission of crimes.

Instigating

179. The Trial Chamber, having already found that the Accused is criminally responsible for aiding and abetting the commission of the crimes in Counts 1-11 of the Indictment, does not find that the Accused also instigated those crimes.

DISPOSITION—The verdict over Charles Taylor.

180. This brings me to the verdict. I will ask the Accused, Charles Ghankay Taylor, to please stand.

181. Having considered all the evidence and the arguments of the parties, the Statute and the Rules, and based upon the findings as determined by the Trial Chamber in its Judgement, the Trial Chamber unanimously finds you guilty of aiding and abetting the commission of the following crimes pursuant to Article 6.1 of the Statute during the Indictment period, and planning the commission of the following crimes in the attacks on Kono and Makeni in December 1998, and in the invasion of and retreat from Freetown between December 1998 and February 1999: 44

Count 1: Acts of terrorism, a violation of Article 3 common to the Geneva Conventions and of Additional Protocol II pursuant to Article 3(d) of the Statute.

Count 2: Murder, a crime against humanity pursuant to Article 2(a) of the Statute.

Count 3: Violence to life, health and physical or mental well-being of persons, in particular murder, a violation of Article 3 common to the Geneva Conventions and of

Additional Protocol II pursuant to Article 3(a) of the Statute.

Count 4: Rape, a crime against humanity, punishable under Article 2(g) of the Statute.

Count 5: Sexual slavery, a crime against humanity, punishable under Article 2(g) of the Statute.

Count 6: Outrages upon personal dignity, a violation of Article 3 common to the Geneva Conventions and of Additional Protocol II pursuant to Article 3(e) of the Statute.

Count 7: Violence to life, health and physical or mental well-being of persons, in particular cruel treatment, a violation of Article 3 common to the Geneva Conventions and of Additional Protocol II pursuant to Article 3(a) of the Statute

Count 8: Other inhumane acts, a crime against humanity pursuant to Article 2(i) of the Statute.

Count 9: Conscripting or enlisting children under the age of 15 years into armed forces or groups, or using them to participate actively in hostilities, another serious violation of international humanitarian law pursuant to Article 4(c) of the Statute. Count 10: Enslavement, a crime against humanity pursuant to Article 2 (c) of the Statute.

Count 11: Pillage, a violation of Article 3 common to the Geneva Conventions and of Additional Protocol II pursuant to Article 3(f) of the Statute.

Did the people of Sierra Leone learn any sense from this?

In conclusion of the above, I don't think even Charles Taylor would have ever had the slightest understanding that he would brought to any court on the surface of the planet earth for questioning by anybody else on earth. He counted very heavily on his diplomatic immunity as a head of state.

However, it is quite enough for any head of state to learn from this lesson that taking advantage on the poor people they rule cannot go unnoticed by the Almighty God who made them and also who give them power to rule over his people? As Charles Taylor is not the only head of state to appear the war crime tribunal in The Hague, has it come to the minds of our current president of Sierra Leone, Earnest Bai Koroma that he is also not exempted from indictment to The Hague in future as he has already started setting the bad example of vote rigging which the whole world has taken notice of under his current rule?

Will another civil war occur again in Sierra Leone?

The answer to this question can only be provided by practicing politicians of today. From our past experience, we have the right to think twice to perceive perception for the future of our country and in the same direction, let me briefly revisit a section of our political history as presented by Rashid Koroma (www.thisissierraleone.com):

Upon returning from the Ruskin College in 1947, where he studied labour relations, Siaka Stevens represented the Sierra Leone People's Party in the Protectorate Assembly, becoming minister of lands, mines, and labour in 1952. After serving as deputy leader of the breakaway People's National Party in 1958 to 1960, he formed his own All People's Congress (APC) in 1960 and was opposition leader from 1961—the year Sierra Leone achieved independence from Britain— until the APC won the 1967 general and presidential elections.

The first general elections under the Republican Constitution were held in 1973, but the elections were marked by violence and political intimidation in which the opposition SLPP withdrew. Stevens introduced the one party rule in 1978 which marked the end of opposition party politics in Sierra Leone and the beginning of all the economic and political instabilies in Sierra Leone.

Siaka Stevens was the architect of all the problems in Sierra Leone today?

President Siaka Stevens ruled Sierra Leone from 1968 to 1985 progressively and consistently undermining the state apparatus thereby destroying public confidence in the state's ability in protecting its people.

The political system which was based on transparency, democracy and the rule of law was no longer trusted by the people under Stevens rule because it was no longer seen as a meaningful political system.

As some political analysts comment, Stevens transformed the already weak democracy into a one party political system, which gave him more power to further corrupt the entire public institutions.

Operating through what Reno (2000: 429) had called a 'shadow State' Stevens and his APC ran the state as a façade, behind which they pursued essentially private forms of political affairs and personal wealth accumulation. Stevens and his men ruled the country through what Reno describes as 'repression', through the military, the police, the judicial apparatuses and the educational system and many of his political rivals were executed.

This frustrated other political opponents and fled the country, thus leading to some extent the beginning of the long and complex civil war that engulfed the entire country.

The army, upon which the state should rely for protection from aggression was seen by the Steven's regime as an obvious threat and therefore he quickly moved to monopolise it. Thus, the regime used the military to suppress the very citizens it was meant to protect.

Atkinson (1998:5) has argued that Stevens' suspicion of a strong military tended to leave the army with largely a ceremonial role in which there were one thousand five hundred professional soldiers plus another one thousand five hundred non-commissioned reservists with little ammunitions and mostly outdated equipments, most of which dated far back to the colonial era.

Major-General Mohammed Tarawallie-the commander of the Sierra Leone army until when the APC government was overthrown in April 1992 by the NPRC frankly confessed in his own words that: 'at the time the rebel war started in March 1991, we were really caught withour pants down'(see Ex-Army Boss Comes Clean, West Africa, 3-9 cited in Keen 2005: 83).

Even recruitment in the military and the police were based not on merit but on what was known as 'connection'. This was done to ensure that the APC regime survived and to be 'violent' in support of the regime if the need arose.

Thus, the Sierra Leonean society was designed in the way that the voices of the poor and the powerless were never heard and Human Rights were best abused, to put it mildly. Intimidation and the disappearance of political opponents and journalists were common and rampant.

The legal system, the security, the education and health systems in Sierra Leone were largely abused and 'put to hell', to put it crudely, which appeared to have fed into the civil war.

The judiciary was weak, corrupt and highly politicized and the poor in particular were always wrongly accused and abused. Prior to the conflict, a joint Department for International Development and World Bank report suggest that the justice system in Sierra Leone operated only effectively for Small number of rich and the powerful elites.

In the wake of World Bank/International Monetary Fund's privatisation scheme that was followed by import-export trade, which the Stevens regime supported did not bring any efficient and competitive market in Sierra Leone, nor did it create a market that could be effectively taxed by the government.

Rather, Stevens and his political allies 'engineered' for themselves key roles in what Keen (1993:75-78) refers to as 'monopolistic'[1] private concerns, using government control over import/export and over the allocation of foreign exchange in favour of their clients and party followers.

In his analysis on corruption and corrupt leadership in Sierra Leone, Sessay (1993:300,309) has argued that the practice of government officials colluding with businessmen (which I am afraid still happens today) to undervalue export embraced the work of multinational companies.

The businessmen who had connection with government officials did not pay correct tax for government goods and taxes were always evaded through the alliances with politicians who will manipulate figures on the quality and quantity of export commodities. In government offices and civil service, bribing for appointment and promotion became 'normal' which Kandeh (1999: 351) describes as 'neo-feudalist formula'.

Thus, increased smuggling in the late 1980s and early 1990s plus the wide spread undervaluing of exports resulted in reducing state revenue very seriously. This caused a major drain on the treasury and in most cases there was less money available for salaries for the country's entire work force.

While education, health and other public sectors were allowed to decline and long term development projects neglected, Stevens' regime continued to give priority to maintaining the royalty to its security service and party supporters.

Steven on state function shortly before he retired from office

The socio-economic and political instability continued well into the 1990s, forcing professional workers such as judges, lawyers and University lecturers to leave the country.

Unemployment rose to the highest level in the country's history undermining the state's economy.

Hirsch (2001:25) and Davies (2000:345) have both argued that Sierra Leone produced US$ 300-US$450 million worth of diamonds annually in the 1980s and 1990s which were apparently smuggled from the country through Liberia and Ivory Coast leaving majority of Sierra Leoneans in extreme poverty.

When the conflict began in 1991, both sides of the conflict-the advancing RUF rebels and the state's military directed their frustration and anger at political leaders for abandoning them to their fate and for squandering the country's resources for their own personal use.

Stevens' iron rule became known as the 'seventeen-year plague of locusts' by his political opponents. His rule destroyed and corrupted every single institutions in the country; parliament was as, his opponents put it 'gutted of significance' in which judges were either intimidate or bribed, the only University (University of Sierra Leone) was starved of funds and many University lecturers compromised their integrity by joining the cabinet, the value of education was deprecated in favour of quick acquisition of wealth and the professionalism of the national army was hugely undermined.

Those who opposed the imposition of one-party state in 1977 for instance, were either executed or forced into exile if they were lucky enough. The thousands of Sierra Leoneans who emigrated to Europe and North America in the 1970s and 1980s left behind a country that was sliding inevitably to the bottom.[2]

More than anything else, Stevens saw himself as an 'embodiment', as the 'neo-patrimonial' ruler[3]and as the 'father of the nation, hence the name 'Pa. Shaki', 'Pass-ar die'. As Boas (2001:708) notes, Stevens' drastic rule spread to all areas of the country's political economy, and the boundaries between the state and private interests deteriorated sharply.

The state's economy was by now controlled by a small group of irresponsible and reckless resident Lebanese traders who collaborated with politicians with Stevens' approval.

Stevens and his 'big men' (as they were known) oversaw a clandestine diamond trade in which diamonds were smuggled out of the country illegally which created what Boas (2001:708-709) has called 'magic money' that helped the political elites to keep the shadow state 'floating'.

It was hoped by the former colonial power—Britain that Sierra Leone would be the model for post-colonial Sub-Saharan African states in economic and political terms.

But the country soon became adrift and exposed to political and economic 'mess-up' characterized by authoritarian rule[4], disrespect for the rule of law, abuse of fundamental Human Rights, rampant corruption and mismanagement which also encouraged tribalism[5].

Thus, only those in power, their tribes' men and families benefited from the government. In effect, politics and economic prospects became a continuous struggle among ethnic groups to achieve regional and tribal hegemony. Thus, patterns of political instability through alternation between civilian authoritarianism and military dictatorship became well established in the post-colonial era.

The country experienced its first military regime in 1967, thereby nurturing the political ambition of the security forces in the national politics which inevitably continued well into the late 1990s (see Abdullah and Mauna 1998:138).

The day Stevens retired from office. By the time he retired from office, he had stolen more than US 500 million of Sierra Leonean money.

Sierra Leone's political record became particularly more chaotic when the country was transformed into a one-party state in 1978 under the leadership of Stevens and his APC party, who ruled for 17 years.

In 1985, Major General Joseph Saidu Momoh who was head of the military succeeded him in what was perceived as undemocratic transition of power, who simply carried forward the bad governance of his predecessor, Stevens.

Despite Momoh's attempt to restoring democratic governance, his efforts were aborted by the outbreak of the civil war in 1991 and a subsequent military coup in 1992, which finally ended the 24-years of one-party authoritarian rule in the country.

The new military regime of the National Provisional Ruling Council (NPRC) initially enjoyed the support of the people but sadly suffered from what experts had called 'pull him down' Syndrome[6].

The successive governments lacked the ability to protect the 'underdeveloped' economy left behind as colonial legacy—and continue to lack the ability to suppress illegal economic activities or to harness the state's resources for significant projects. Successive government officials built their fortunes and power-base through the use of patronage and intimidation and the mineral rich country remains one of the poorest in the world.

It is evidence that the conflict and the atrocities committed during the war periods are the consequence of years of ruthlessness and mismanagement by political and economic elites that forced the entire nation to experience socio-economic and political breakdown.

Since the conflict emerged within the context of a deeply dysfunctional and corrupt neo-patrimonial system, it can therefore be argued that the political and economic problems of Sierra Leone did not start today or just yesterday. It started well back in the 1970s and worse particularly in the 1980s under the Momoh regime, which altogether underpinned the civil war that lasted for well over ten years.

Economic mismanagement of Sierra Leone during Siaka Stevens rule

Sierra Leone's economic resources were abused and grossly mismanaged dating far back to the late 1970s and 1980s. Sierra Leone blessed with natural endowment including diamonds; one of the most resourced rich countries in Africa remains one of the poorest nations in the world.

Some available evidence suggests that the country's main economic source of income has been its mineral deposit particularly diamonds (Davies 2000:354).

Thus, it is increasingly worrying that Sierra Leone never actually managed to organize its own economy. Part of the problems lies in the mismanagement of its diamond proceeds that provides by far the most significant of readily available wealth. As Bangura (2000:555) comments, diamond resources has been, and still is very difficult to bring under control by the state given its component worth [7].

At least one evidence (Davies 2000:559) suggests that during colonial rule, mining activities were carried out by one multinational corporation—the Sierra Leone Selection Trust (SLST).

The 'monopoly' of the trust includes the control of capital and technical skills and was also in control of large scale of potentially diamond bearing areas; the main concentration being Kono, and Tongo in the east[8].

In 1971, under the leadership of President Stevens, the state's own National Diamond Mining Company (NDMC) took over the SLST because of what Davies (2000:353) describes as massive theft of state diamonds by the Stevens regime. At this time, the diamond industry was controlled by Jamil Said Mohammed (Stevens' business ally and his best friend).

The Stevens government allowed him to control the commercial linkage between small dealers and the state on one hand, and between the state and the larger global diamond market on the other. He also maintained political linkages between the country's main source of cash and the network of prominent corruptible politicians. The state's inability to collect revenue from the diamond sector was on the increase which caused the national economy to deteriorate at a faster rate.

By mid 1980s, the process of unlawful diamond mining throughout the country has made the state institutions to collapse particularly the NDMC. This brought corporate mining to an end forcing the Sierra Leonean society into what Reno (2000:130) and Kandeh (2002:2) had called a 'free for all' mining system[9].

As Reno (2000:130) highlights, Stevens himself is said to have stolen an estimated US$500 million of Sierra Leonean money, leaving a balance of only US$ 196,000 in foreign reserves on the day he retired from office.

These plus Stevens' non-essential economic and 'prestige projects', the unfortunate global oil crisis in 1973 which coincided with the declined of diamond and iron ore prices, plus the dwindling revenues compounded by governmental corruption and lavish spending escalated the economic decline in the country.

This turned the country from being the model for democratic governance and economic prosperity in the sub region to what Reno (1995:198) called the 'exemplar' of Africa's postcolonial neo-patrimonial malaise[10]where the country's wealth were redistributed to party followers and supporters, leaving the rest of the population with little to eat.

To make the matter worst and a complete state failure in Sierra Leone, Stevens' ambition to be popular among other corrupt African leaders, he 'bankrupted' the country's crippling economy by hosting the annual summit of the Organization of African Unity (OAU) now the African Unity (AU).

Stevens was to become the chairman of the summit and hence the 'leader of Africa'. In an attempt to persuade Stevens that it was not necessary to host the summit and therefore it was a waste of money, thugs acting on the president's order executed Bangura—the then governor of the Bank of Sierra Leone by ejecting him from his three storey building in 1979 (For more analysis on Bangura, see also Reno 1999:16).

This forced other politicians who had wanted to protest against the summit to flee the country. About one year following the summit, the government was unable to pay its workers and its external debt. As Hirsch (2001:29-30) notes, about a year's state spending was as he put it 'wasted' on the summit which left the educational system, the health services, the justice system, the security and other institutions to degrade at a very faster rate.

This was and still is the way most African leaders are irresponsible, corrupt and wasteful [11].

When political liberalization accompanies economic reforms especially where it is being handled by unreliable corruptible foreign firms, tax evasion is always the case. When for instance, the Sierra Leone government welcomed SCIPA, an Israeli mining firm to mine diamonds in 1989 under the Momoh government, the official agreement was to raise official diamond export and to assist in Sierra Leone's payment of arrears to the IMF.

Reno (1995: 209) has noted that in the bid for SCIPA to gain the contract, Nir Guaz—the head of the company paid some civil servants who were close to the president a huge sum of money in the form of bribe.

Most politicians and particularly those who were closed to the president also had free access to large amounts of mining plots and therefore had easier access to foreign exchange independent of the president's favour.

In addition, Guaz tapped into illicit diamond operations controlled by 'strong men' who contested the president's authority (see West Africa 25 February 1991: 268 cited in Reno 1995: 207 and 208).

Sierra Leone's ironic tragedy suggest that where there is bad political leadership, political and civil institutions become weak and thus, endowment of 'lootable' natural resources such as diamonds and timber can be a curse and not a blessing to a nation whose leaders are ready to offer little economic benefits to its citizens.

The unequal benefit arising from the country's resources and the inability of the state authorities to adequately tax the sales of natural resources were and still remains part of the wider problems affecting all economic activities from Sierra Leone, which underpins institutional frigidity that led to the conflict and complete state failure.

This also explains the unequal trading relationships and of corrupt government officials who were and are always ready to collide with smuggling and undervaluing the state's exports.

Blaming the RUF, the Sierra Leone military, the Kamajors, external factors, mercenaries, international institutions and other warlords such as Charles Taylor for their parts in the civil war and for institutional failure in Sierra Leone, it is equally important to blame patrimonial politics, greed, corruption and bad governance of the Siaka Stevens and the subsequent regimes for the strategic state failure which have led to all the problems that our country is going through today.

In his 17 years of miss-rule, Stevens had the opportunity to put many things in place which the people of our nation would have enjoyed today.

Note:

----

[1] Bradbury (1995:22) has noted that the interference of government ministers into the market sector further degraded the formal taxable economy, which allowed private companies with powerful political allies to avoid taxation at the same time allowing smuggling to escalate to the highest degree under the nose of Stevens.

[2] Some available United Nations statistics suggest that by the early 1990s, Sierra Leone was, and still is among the poorest countries in the world with majority of its people living on less than one dollar a day regardless of its ample natural resources.

[3] Boas (2001:708) has noted that Stevens saw himself as the head of the extended Sierra Leonean family by claiming roots in all major ethnic groups in the country and by cultivating the picture of himself-'Pa Siakie'—meaning the father of the nation.

[4] See Zack-Williams (1999)

[5] In his annual national speech in 1989, president Momoh urged all his subjects to form themselves into ethnic cabals. By then, power had already shifted from parliament and the cabinet to the Ekutay—Momoh's tribal cabal. This further worsens ethnic relations and speed economic decline (see Zack-Williams 1999:146).

[6]During the war periods, most Sierra Leoneans particularly the marginalized youths believed that some politicians have in the past spoilt much of the country's resources for so long and they were therefore ready and willing to 'spoilt all' and then fix it later.

[7] Sierra Leone's diamonds can easily be extracted without much complications or much use of heavy machineries as in other places like South Africa, where deep excavations are required.

[8] It is estimated that 70% of Sierra Leonean diamonds are concentrated along the kimberlite starting from the Kambui hills in Kenema District through Tongo into Kono District in the East.

[9] Some evidence including (Kandeh 2002:1-4) has argued that Jamil Sahid Mohammad and others were responsible for the massive

diamond theft belonging to the state, and yet he remains the 'bosom' man and best friend of the president.

[10] Of particular importance to Stevens regime was the distribution of heavily subsidized rice and other goods to the army, the police and other security services. This caused a major strain on the economy, with always less money available for salaries which increased reliance on Stevens' handout.

[11] In his analysis on the hosting of the OAU (now AU) summit in Sierra Leone in 1980, Clapham (2003:13) has argued that Stevens' desperation to be seen as the 'leader of Africa' led to 'dubious' deals with dubious businessmen and other foreign investors which includes secret arrangements for the storage of toxic waste products in Sierra Leone.

Having revisited our political history, especially under Siaka Stevens rule of APC party from 1967 to 1985 (18years), one can see clearly that under one dictator's rule for eighteen years followed by Joseph Saidu Momoh's rule from 1985 to 1992(7years) which in total amounted to 25 years of APC rule was not a style of politics accepted by majority of the entire population of Sierra Leone; until APC got kicked out by National Provisional Ruling Council (NPRC) through a military coup, but engineered by the civil war which was already in progress. Let us remember that my brother, Foday Sankoh stated from day one of the civil war that his intention was to kick APC out of power. He therefore succeeded when the military boys, headed by Valentine Strasser, completed his mission.

Now, let me come back to the question "Will there be another civil war in Sierra Leone?" Let me say again that the answer to that question lays in the hands of current practicing politicians, especially those on the side of the All Peoples Congress (APC) under President Ernest Bai Koroma who is now running for the second term. Let me please congratulate him for the political victory at this time (even though under mischievous circumstances) emanating from the office of the National Electoral Commission, Dr. Christiana Thorpe.

If he refuses to go at the end of his term of rule in 2017 or if he undermines the political system, possibly in collaboration with the National Electoral Commission (NEC) again for ensuring the APC control of government, let him just remember that he will be provoking the second phase of the Sierra Leone civil war. Ernest Koroma and all members of the APC political party must understand that other political parties in Sierra Leone have the right to rule and the people of Sierra Leone have the right to elect their leaders <u>free and fair</u>. We are fed up of a system whereby only a coup d'état can remove a government. It is about time when all political parties in Sierra Leone, especially those in power to begin to think of human developments through education. When priority is paid to educating the people of a nation, the spill over effects result in their abilities to emerge with tremendous areas of developments for themselves and their county without too much reliant on their governments'.

What is more disgusting about Ernest Koroma's government is the neglect of education in favour of lousy projects of road building to create public impression to show that he is doing well for the country; when in fact these roads are time timed-longed with timed durability when he knows very well that he may not be living at the time the life span of the roads come to maturity for servicing.

However Ernest Koroma's neglect of education in Sierra Leone at this point in time may not come as a surprise because one of the APC Foundation Stones laid by Siaka Stevens was not to look at education with any form of dignity, but to in fact to press down on education so that the highly educated élite cannot become "bones in his throat".

As he was not a university educated graduate, despite the Certificate in Trade Unionism he completed at Ruskin College in Oxford, UK.

"Den say Bailor-Barry, you say Koso-Thomas?" became a common mockery in the country (comparing the currupt diamond magnet with the highest academic) during his reign.

Ernestst Koroma's government has gradually 'derecognised' the service of teachers in Sierra Leone such that they have become worthless and so looked down upon in a way such that they are even unable to afford living in comfort accommodations in the country, not mentioning decent salaries and even the meagre salaries of teachers are delayed to the point of three months before getting half; these educated people ere mandated in their work roles to appear decently in front of their students they teach. Teachers salary delays have encouraged many teachers to live on printing and selling pamphlets to their students as well as attending their private lessons without which their students have no chance of passing their examinations. Who is responsible for this corruption, is it the teachers or Koroma's Ministry of Education? What they do is to create blames on educational institutions for their calamities such as the articles that I came across published by Brima Michael Turay, PRO for Ministry of Education.

Times Newspaper in Freetown, Sierra Leone.

What May Cause a Delay in Paying Teachers' Salary?

By Brima Michael Turay: PRO—Ministry of Education Science and Technology

Mar 28, 2013, 17:06

Email this article

Printer friendly page

Anytime there is a delay in payment of Teachers' Salaries, the public raises eye brows at the Ministry of Education and blames the government for not doing enough to effect payments in a timely manner.

Teachers, unlike Lecturers, are recruited by the Ministry of Education and the timely payment of their salaries is usually facilitated by the Ministry of Education. We would therefore like to inform the public that it is not all delays in payment of salaries that is caused by the Ministry of Education.

As a matter of fact, the Ministry is hardly responsible for delays in Teacher salary payments; and where the Ministry is directly responsible, it has always endeavoured to rectify the situation before it becomes intolerable. Up until 2006, what used to happen was that at the start of every school year Principals and Headmasters of schools would recruit Teachers to fill all vacant teaching positions in their respective schools pending approval for payment of salaries for such recruitment by the Accountant General through the Ministry of Education.

The Principals and Headmasters would then submit the application forms for these new recruits to the Ministry of Education for verification and to facilitate the approval process. The verification process usually takes time because the Ministry of Education wants to make sure they are not recruiting **"Ghost Teachers"** into the system.

Other factors like late submission of verifiable documentation by new recruits or slight discrepancies in degrees and Certificates may also contribute to the delays. Consequently, for most Teachers, the delay may drag for a year or more without approval by the Ministry of Education.

Some Principals and Headmasters, in a bid to retain the newly recruited Teachers, would give out loans to the new recruits with the hope of deducting such loans from their salaries when the salaries are finally approved.

Brima M. Turay—PRO—Ministry of Education

By 2006, upon the recommendation of our donor partners, since our economy is mostly donor-driven, a moratorium was placed on recruiting new Teachers into the School system. The rationale was that the donor partners and the government would like to know how many Teachers are in the system so as to enhance a culture of transparency and accountability.

Therefore, from 2006 to this present moment, the Ministry of Education would only approve the replacement of Teachers. If a School loses a Teacher, that particular school is mandated to replace the said Teacher by submitting the relevant documentation to the Ministry of Education through the Directorate office.

The Ministry would then send the documentation of the outgoing Teacher and all relevant information of the incoming Teacher to the Accountant General at the Ministry of Finance. Once the information is verified and the Accountant General is fully satisfied with all the information supplied, the name of the new Teacher is then reflected on the payment voucher and the **"Pin Code"** by which the outgoing Teacher is normally identified is expunged from the system by the Accountant General and a new **"Pin Code"** is generated for the new Teacher to avoid duplicity in payments.

Sometimes the delay is not only caused by these necessary bureaucracies at the Ministries of Education and Finance but simply by the negligence of certain Principals and Headmasters in the manner in which they handle Teacher salary documentation and late submission of salary documentation before the deadline of the 9th day of every month. A typical example of such negligence could be found in a recent MEMO from the Accountant General at the Ministry of Finance to the Ministry of Education with a list of names of Schools that have not submitted a breakdown of how they expended the previous salary allocations for the period October 2012 to February 2013. Such breakdown is usually dubbed as **"RETURNS"**; or **"Reconciliation Documents"**. It is a common practice of sound accounting principles that before the Accountant General issues out a new cheque (Check) or pay voucher to any school Principal or Headmaster for Teachers' salaries; the previous disbursement must be fully accounted for through acceptable documentation (**RETURNS**).

The Ministry of Education would therefore like the public to know that several schools in the North, East and Southern regions of the country have not submitted the said **"RETURNS"** at the stipulated time and could possibly experience delays in payment of salaries to Teachers in the schools so affected. The Ministry would also like the public to know that all Principals and Headmasters are aware of the deadline and have been sufficiently notified prior. Here is a breakdown, in a tabular form, of schools in Provinces and Districts that would be affected by this unfortunate situation:

Number of Primary and Secondary Schools that will be affected

Province	District	
Northern	Kambia	5
	Bombali	3
	Tonkolili	4
	Koinadugu	2
	Port Loko	2
Southern	Bo	21
	Pujehun	11
	Moyamba	10
	Bonthe	2
Eastern	Kenema	107
	Kailahun	24
	Kono	35
Total Schools		**226**

Approximately 226 schools across the country are going to be affected by this anomaly caused by their Principals or Headmasters. This revelation is not intended to set the Teachers against their Principals or Headmasters but the Ministry has a responsibility to inform the public about any discrepancies that may possibly put the Ministry on the spotlight and consequently draw scorn and disdain from the public; particularly from the Teachers that will soon be affected. The Ministry, as part of its responsibility, and through its Directorate office, has notified the schools so affected through their Principals and Headmasters. The Ministry further wants the public to know that it is fully committed to ensuring that Teachers across the country receive their salaries on time as soon as the current **"Cleaning Up"** exercise is completed. The recent recruitment of over 70 Inspectors of Schools will facilitate the speedy conclusion of this **"Cleaning exercise"**. We want to thank all Teachers, Principals and Headmasters across the country for the numerous sacrifices that they make every day to improve our standard of education in the face of great challenges.

Please Note:

Pity enough teaching profession in my country is no longer prioritised by government Ministry of Education since 2006 but by donor partners when millions are spent on road construction with no attention paid to teachers who are trained to contribute towards national developments through education, according to this press release of Ernest Bai Koroma's Ministry of Education.

Although Ernest Bai Koroma is embarked upon infrastructure relating to road construction around the country, that is not the priority need of the people of Sierra Leone who elected him in power. Let him focus attention on "Peoples Development Projects" through the provision of educational facilities, so that when Sierra

Leonean children are well educated, starting with looking after teachers well be encouraging teachers to feel good and become proud of their career and this feed good factor will motivate majority of those they teach to begin to think of planning to become teachers in future. Koroma was thought by a teacher on the very day he went to attend primary school. He went through many teachers, through out primary, secondary schools and till he finished university of education at Fourah B ay College; all engineered by teachers. It is therefore very ungrateful to stir his government to treat teachers in this country in the way they are now treated. This totally not fair but cruel and evil.

MOHAMED SANNOH's PRAYER and ADVICE TO POLITICIANS IN SIERRA LEONE.

"Personally, I will continue to pray that everlasting peace remains in Sierra Leone and also that we do not go over civil unrest again, especially through civil war. But for this prayer to be answered, our politicians and our political machineries have to shape the political movements decently in the way such that all participants should have a very decent breathing space. All Sierra Leoneans have right to participate in the politics of Sierra Leone without victimisation of any sort from ruling party"

I am beginning to think that our politicians and our political machineries are still yet to learn from experience. Remember that the civil war we all suffered from did not start over night but it was at first sewn by Siaka Stevens as explained already in this book.

CHAPTER NINE

Dr. Christian Thorpe's Press Release and action for vote rigging

Is Dr.Christiana Thorpe, Head of Electoral Commission of Sierra Leone corrupt?

We all saw the recent election that took place September 2012. The international observers say that it was a clean election that went free and fair; but certain question still remains in my mind unanswered. The electoral commissioner Dr Christiana Thorpe was placed in charge to oversee the election process and I personally congratulate her boldness to do the job. She had the right in her capacity to disqualify any vote in any constituency where she suspected any form of foul play, but her press release before the final election results was as follows:

PRESS RELEASE BY CEC / CHAIRPERSON ON UPDATE OF ELECTION RESULTS TALLYING AT REGIONAL TALLY CENTERS—TUESDAY 21ST, NOVEMBER, 2012

UPDATE ON ELECTION RESULTS TALLYING AT REGIONAL TALLY CENTERS,(PDF VERSION)

Dr. Christiana A. M. Thorpe

Chief Electoral Commissioner / Chairperson

National Returning Officer

    A. Response To Concerns From PMDC and SLPP

The Commission received concerns from both the Peoples Movement of Democratic Change (PMDC) and the Sierra Leone Peoples Party (SLPP) pertaining to the conduct of elections and performance of NEC staff and other security personnel on polling day.

The Commission will like to point out the following:
Missing Final Voter Register in several polling stations in Bombali and Koinadugu
Bombali-We are aware that voter register for one centre was misplaced but was later found in another centre within the same ward.

Koinadugu—the election procedure allows for the generation of the register based on the presentation of a voter ID where the original register was not available on polling day. This was what occurred in Koinadugu and in any other area where it was found necessary to do so.

Interference by certain NEC officials in voters' choice selection
We would like the political parties to provide any evidence in their possession to the police.

Ballot Stuffing and Intimidation etc.

NEC has not announced the results of any individual constituency or centre therein. We can therefore not comment on the allegations regarding this issue.

We have no reports of NEC official being put under gun point. Any evidence of this should be provided to the police.

NEC cannot comment on the supply of electricity to polling station save to say that polling kits include alternative source of light.

Kassel Farm—We will ask that more specific information be given to the police.

St Edwards Secondary School—we have received no report of any NEC official being arrested for any such incident. Further NEC cannot comment on whether there was a curfew in the area as it is outside its mandate.

Refusal by NEC Officials to give out party Agents RRFs
There was a shortage of original RRFs in some parts of the country which affected all parties. However NEC officials used observer copies which were posted outside the centers.

Evidence of Unsigned or unstamped RRFs
In relation to this issue NEC observed this lapse and where it occurred investigations have been carried out to verify the results. It is important to understand that all who voted must have their votes counted and no one should feel disenfranchised.

NEC Officials directing voters to vote Ernest Koroma

In response to this matter, we advise that this information be given to the police.

RRFs not signed

Any information relating to RRF not signed should be referred to the police and please keep NEC informed. NEC is surprised to learn that party agents could sign blank RRFs thereby colluding in wrong doing.

People without Voter IDs and not on the voter register allowed to vote. This is a matter for the police and they should be provided with the necessary evidence.

64 Ballot boxes quarantined

We do not have a system wherein ballot boxes are quarantined. Generally tampered envelopes are quarantined pending investigations.

We request that any evidence of irregularity at Buxton School and elsewhere be reported to the police.

UPDATE ON ELECTION RESULTS TALLYING AT REGIONAL TALLY CENTERS

The Commission hereby wishes to inform the general public that 99% of all polling stations results have now being received at the Regional Tally Centers in Kenema, Makeni, Bo and Freetown. Out of the 9,493 polling stations, 90% of (8,544) polling station results have been processed. The

Remaining 10% of polling station results have been quarantined and may require opening of affected ballot boxes and recount of the ballot papers.

The Commission strongly condemns the use of copies of the Final Voters Register (FVR) by political party agents on polling day to undertake parallel voter verification. The Commission distributed the FVR to the political parties for their internal use and not to undertake any parallel identification or verification of voters, thereby obstructing the electoral process and infringing of the privacy of voters.

All vehicles with stickers marked NEC operations used on polling day with the exception of security vehicles should now be removed with immediate effect

Signed:
Dr. Christiana Thorpe
Chief Electoral Commissioner/Chairperson
National Returning Officer <http://www.facebook.com/email_open_log_pic.php?c=739658650&mid=7173db1G5af3b9c7a829G348b38dG96>

The analysis that this press release left us with was that, there was already some level of disagreement she knew very well about before the result was released but it appears that she had already compromised in the interest of certain candidates which could leave her no alternative but to accept vote rigging.

If she was not ready to interfere, why did she not use her mandatory power as the National Electoral Commissioner to cancel election votes in constituencies where there were doubts about events that could be considered as vote rigging?

Was Dr. Christiana Thorpe under any form of duress pressure or threats from anybody to direct the votes in the interest and for the winning of any particular political party? I am seriously afraid but to arrive at the point that Dr. Christiana Thorpe, the National Electoral Commission for the 2012 Presidential election of my country, the Republic of Sierra Leone compromised to a high level percentage in vote rigging in favour of the winning party.

This is corruption in the highest degree within the political machinery of Sierra Leone. It appears that she was reassured that nothing will happen to her and that nobody will even ask her any form of question. Above all, she has been given body guard securities to look after her always as she even now carries some around her as I write this book.

Is it another chapter of African politics still opened in front of Sierra Leoneans to learn from? Is she also assuring of Diplomatic Immunity that Charles Taylor of Liberia was banking on until he was finally prosecuted in The Hague? This seed of corruption is sewn to germinate into civil conflict in Sierra Leone even if it is in the long run. The international community has already taken note of this and I am sure that time will come one day when she will be asked these questions by powers of authority of the law to provide answers to.

May God help us all in Sierra Leone.

CHAPTER TEN

What are the origins of Africa's civil conflicts?

Putting the answer to this question straight, the origins of Africa's civil conflicts are the very corrupt politicians who think that members of the civil society are just very stupid and do not take note of the corruptions they do and there is nothing they can do even if they are discovered. We are Sierra Leoneans and have strong hope in God the Almighty. Nobody in any power capacity can seize advantage of Sierra Leoneans and get away with it. The former president of Charles Taylor will ever remain to regret why he misused his power on Sierra Leoneans as it was revealed in The Hague. The power of Diplomatic Immunity under which evil politicians hide is always revocable whenever the time arrives. It is about time for all of us to learn from this fact.

What are the solutions to Africa's Civil Conflicts?

In as much as African countries do not like conflicts, is still unavoidable, meaning that conflicts still do occur in addition to causes of politicians' corruption, especially in our country Sierra Leone. Human life is always affected by conflicts that attack from different directions and at most of the time when these conflicts are not prepared for and thus unexpected by many. Those who prepare for conflicts and expect them at anytime are the corrupt politicians' who do not care about the effects of civil conflicts on a nation. Corrupt politicians are not even sensitive about how people of particular tribe feel about the unbalanced of their political activities when they are in power.

They always feel that it is their own time to enjoy even when their enjoyment is at the detriment of other people who are equally citizens of the same country. They feel that it is time for their children to get educational sponsorships, it is time for their areas to get good roads, good hospitals, electivity supply, good drinking water facilities, and so on. They just do not care.

When this kind of "damned attitudes" continues for the second or third term of office of the same political leader, the tribes and areas of this deprivation will begin to cry out loud to their government about their sufferings and where sometimes no listening ear is given to them, they will start to take other person that breathes on the planet earth.

Once again, let me emphasise here that conflict is hardly unavoidable even between husbands and wives, brothers and sisters, workers within, teachers and students, nations and nations and so on. When misunderstanding, especially politically related, breaks out between tribes or population of a country that leads to civil conflicts (within the same country), there is always a reason for that and the solutions that bring such conflicts are approached in many ways that are as follows:

i. The offended always try in their humanly way possible to approach their Member of Parliament (MP) for the information of their head of state and demand that their MP reports back to them within a specific period of time.

ii. If their MP reports back to them with negative respond from the head of state, that community is opened to the strategy of organising themselves for a delegation to approach their head of state with preparations of complaining points by points, to the full understanding of the head of state of what is happening that they do not like. It then remains the honours of that head of state to take them seriously after receiving the same complaints from the MP followed by a delegation of their community members. ***Please understand that politics in general is***

always a population alarm game and all politicians including heads of states take seriously any community that learns the strategy of playing this political game as their politicians will begin to see the after effects in camera.

iii. Where the incidents continues beyond repairs to point that the head of state is seen as giving deaf ears by not taking appropriate actions to end their calamities, the tendency will be either **"to sit quietly on time bomb"** to wait for an individual who is bold enough to start a rebellious group in the country for which many followers are patronised or the community boldly takes the law into their own hands, as a group through fighting to fix things correctly. Therefore what the community has initially trying to prevent from braking out into civil conflicts now gradually is becoming civil war for which the head of state now has no control over.

I have no hesitation here to state that it is only a stupid and evil head of state that cannot see civil wars coming on the road before they arrives finally in their country for which they themselves will seriously suffer. Once civil war is in a country, the head of state of that country, including all his cabinet ministers are troubled in their minds for twenty-four-hours a day, meaning that they have no chance to sleep well and have personal pleasures as human beings. Therefore, why should corrupt politicians in Africa sow seeds of civil conflicts in their countries? The solution to civil conflicts is not straightforward as people may think but there are different alternatives to chose from:

a. The head of state to look into matters seriously and acknowledge where some parties have gone wrong against others and bring all such parties together to address them openly (not in secret).

b.   To demand apology from those parties that have wrongfully affected others and pledges some community supports for the affected areas (such as building of bridges, constructing decent water supply facility, local school) etc. Thereafter, the head of state will pay visits to the affected community to reassure them with their important roles in the country and his continuous support for their community buildings.

Sometimes, civil conflicts in Africa can go beyond solutions of country's heads of states. This is where the civil conflicts escalate into civil war and at that level; the head of state is longer respected as a negotiator to warring parties and those who listen to him will only be putting themselves at the risks of having them killed. At this point the solutions become diverse and some of which are not appreciable by human nature and these solutions are listed as follows:

1.   *Supply more weapons to government soldiers and also to other fighters (opposition to government fighters) so that they will continue shooting and killing each other in the country until they **all die**. When that happens those who were able to flee the war into asylum in other countries during the war as well as citizens of the country who have already left years before the war are returned to rebuild their country and live peacefully ever after.*

2.   *Some reasonable sober minded elements from both sides of the conflict meet and analyse where the war is heading and accept that they have both wronged*

each other and decides to invite independent parties from outside for a peace negotiation talk aiming at ending the conflict. This is where the United Nations Organisations (UNO) comes in; but the problem with the UN now-a-days is that almost all nationalities in the world have some level of connections in the UN and there is always bias side to support in such civil conflicts talks.

Sometimes this bias supports are helpful as it happens in the Sierra Leone Civil war. Tejan Kabbah, no doubt had a lot of contact supports from Kofi Anan with whom he had earlier on work for years at the UN. One can recall that Sierra Leone had the largest peace keeping military supports from the UN to assist with peace keeping in the civil war of Sierra Leone. Such support did not come ordinarily without Tejan Kabbah's solicited support from Kofi Anan.

The Lome Peace Conference for which President Kabbah went into power sharing with my brother, Foday Sankoh is one of the incidents that cannot be forgotten during solutions to civil war years in Sierra Leone.

Final warning

As far as my analysis of incidents that led to Sierra Leone civil war, Siaka Stevens gave deaf ears to many sufferings in many different communities in Sierra Leone and used political powers to bully them out.

One typical example I can collect was when the people of Koya chiefdom in Kenema District rebelled against the paramount chief Momoh Kanneh-iii for cannibalism in which a fifteen year old girl, Lucy Kamboima was killed and her parts removed in a bush at

Lowoma in the Koya Chiefdom. The pathology reports of Dr. Oju Mends who was the senior pathologist in Sierra Leone revealed traces of cannibalism. In fact the incidence was witnessed by a very small boy, who was going to toilet in the bush at the time the group arrived with the girl. He waited in hiding patiently and watched all of their activities until the act were done and the group left.

When the matter finally reached Siaka Stevens, for final decision and punishments for all those involved, he swept it under the carpet, leaving such allegation investigated, for the simple fact that E.T. Kamara who was the Secretary General of APC Party was married to Jeneba Kallon, cousin of the Paramount Chief Momoh Kanneh-iii.

Similar blanket supports for APC supporters in different parts of the country went on for long, during Siaka Steven presidency over Sierra Leone. **"As long as you were APC supporter, you can commit murder and get away with it"**. That was APC Party, as far as I can recall in those days in Sierra Leone and all such political records amount to civil war in the country, even when Siaka Stevens died.

If President Ernest Bai Koroma is intelligent enough, it is about time to begin to think that the longer APC or any other political party stays in power in Sierra Leone, the higher, the tension mounts for leadership change and the more people become dissatisfied with party supporters activities, some of which the head of state may not be even aware of.

Therefore, I appeal to the president to treat everybody equally and fairly in the distribution of the country's meagre resources especially in education all provisions. If I were in his position, I will spend eighty percent of government budget, in three main areas and these are: **Education! Education! and Education.**

You are not the president of APC party but the president of all Sierra Leoneans including those who did not vote for the All Peoples Congress (APC) party in Sierra Leone.

Ernest must understand that until all Sierra Leoneans are educated, problems in our country will never end and we may be heading for another civil war in this country. Another civil war can be avoided by encouraging teachers through prompt payments of their salaries; every month.

As you are already planning to stay in office after the end of your second term, I would just like to remind you that the day you plan stay for another term, could be the day of commencement of the second phase of the Sierra Leone civil war and you will ever remain to regret for igniting that.

APC's Third Term is Still Firmly on Track in Sierra Leone

By

May 10, 2013, 17:20   Email this article   Printer friendly page

You May Click Here To Read or
Discuss Views About This Article

APC's Third Term is still firmly on track as there is no Constitutional Limit on how many times a political party can win presidential elections in Sierra Leone. However it should be noted that a President himself can serve no more than two terms . . . **SEE BELOW**

OFFICE OF THE PRESIDENT STATE HOUSE, FREETOWN

PRESS RELEASE

It has come to the notice of Government that certain individuals are peddling rumours that His Excellency the President, Dr. Ernest Bai Koroma intends to run for a third term as President of the Republic of Sierra Leone. This is totally untrue and against the provision of the 1991 National Constitution which stipulates the tenure of President and restricts such tenure to two consecutive terms only. Whoever is circulating the rumour is doing so out of ignorance or over-zealousness.

The rumour threatens to undermine the democratic credentials of President Koroma, as such rumours stand at variance with the thinking of His Excellency the President who has on many occasions made it very clear that he is not interested in a third term of office.

This rumour should not be allowed to interfere with the present moves by Government to review the 1991 National Constitution, because the review will not interfere with the Presidential term limit, as stipulated in the constitution.

The co-operation of the General Public is most vital in Government's efforts to modernize state governance which will be incorporated in a revised constitution that will address vital aspects relating to human rights, gender and youth issues, and the rule of law.

It should be emphasized that President Ernest Bai Koroma will run his second term of office in full and any effort to divert his attention from efforts to further develop the country will be resisted.

At the moment, there is no room for any debate on the tenure of office of the President as this is clearly entrenched in the provisions of the Constitution of Sierra Leone.

Dated 9th May, 2013.

ALL THE TIME, JESUS CHRIST REMAINS IN CONTROL OF SIERRA LEONE AND EVERY SIERRA LEONEAN IS BLESSED.

Mohamed Sannoh

Member of Sierra Leone Teachers Union.

www.ingramcontent.com/pod-product-compliance
Lightning Source LLC
Chambersburg PA
CBHW020524290526
45786CB00002B/753